LYN

ROLL ON THE RODNEY

Also by David Phillipson

Smuggling, a History
Band of Brothers, Boy Seamen in the Royal Navy 1800–1956

To the sailors of the old Navy,
who endured it.

This is my story, this is my song:
Been in commission far too long;
Roll on the Rodney, Nelson, Renown,
This (three-funnelled/flat-topped etc.) bastard is getting me down!

(To the well-known hymn tune)

ROLL ON THE RODNEY

David Phillipson

SUTTON PUBLISHING

First published in 1999 by
Sutton Publishing Limited · Phoenix Mill
Thrupp · Stroud · Gloucestershire · GL5 2BU

British Library Cataloguing in Publication Data
A catalogue record for this book is available from the British Library

ISBN 0 7509 1968-X

 TM   ALAN SUTTON™ and SUTTON™ are the
trade marks of Sutton Publishing Limited

Typeset in 10/12pt Baskerville
Typesetting and origination by
Sutton Publishing Limited
Printed in Great Britain by
WBC Ltd, Bridgend

Contents

Illustrations

Plates

Between pages 56 and 57

Acknowledgements

No book of this kind could be written without the help of very many people, and this I have received in generous measure. At various times over a year and a half I placed appeals on Channel 4 Teletext, in *Navy News*, the Royal Navy's newspaper, and in the HMS *Ganges* Association's Gazette. All proved fruitful, and my grateful thanks go to their respective editors for allowing me use of their pages.

I want to thank all those ex-Navy men, many from the Commonwealth, who responded so unstintingly to my appeals and made this book possible. They not only wrote or telephoned with their stories but were eager to enlarge upon them as I might require and in many cases, offered to lend their precious photographs. I can only list them here by name, in alphabetical order rather than by the size of individual contributions, including those whose offerings through lack of space or to avoid duplication I had reluctantly to leave out. I hope I have included every respondent in the following list and ask forgiveness of anyone omitted:

A. Allcock, R. Anderson, D. Banks, R. Bennett BEM, M. Bree, R. Brookes, G. Bullock, J. Crew, J. Christison, G. Curtis, L. Dennis, A. Dickinson, J. Ellis, W. Fleckney, D. Giles, D. Goodall, R. Grevett, J. Grisman, D. Harding, E. Harris, C. Harrold, R. Harwood, V. Hocking, R. Jamieson, G. Jay, D. Jones, J. Leach, D. Macfarlane, J. McIntyre, H. Male, K. Moore, L. Mossop, K. Norton, J. Owen, R. Owen, R. Palmer, K. Parker, A. Perrett, F. Phillips, J. Roche, J. Smith, C. Steven ISO, C. Taylor, C. Tonkin, N. Townsley, J. Huntington-Whitely VRD, B. Whitworth, G. Whybrow, P. Wilkins, F. Woods, E. Wyatt, A. Zammit.

My grateful thanks go to Max Arthur and to Mr Anthony Wells, son of the late Capt. John Wells, for permission to include passages from their respective books which are listed in the bibliography. Thanks also to John Morris, whose excellent warship drawings adorn the text, and to Lesley Taylor, for allowing me use of her facilities. Finally to Jonathan Falconer and Helen Gray of Sutton's, for seeing it through to publication.

DJP, Biggin by Hulland
Derbyshire
September 1998

Introduction

The years immediately after the end of the Second World War, with Great Britain embarking upon the long, painful process of shedding her imperial role, were difficult ones for the Royal Navy. *Pax Britannica* was replaced by the newly-formed North Atlantic Treaty Organization dominated by a powerful United States Navy, inheritor of Britannia's trident. Britain, impoverished by the war, had perforce to make stringent economies, not least in her armed services. A Labour government imposed cuts in naval manpower and resources which alarmed traditionalists and added to the Navy's difficulties in recruiting and retaining personnel of the calibre needed in a new technological age, against the competition of high wages and full employment ashore.

It was also a time of higher expectations on the lower deck with regard to living conditions on board ship and to conditions of service generally. Many regular ratings had not failed to notice, during the war and since, the immeasurably superior shipboard facilities enjoyed by their US Navy counterparts – bunks to sleep in, cafeterias to eat in and much better quality and choice of food; onboard bakeries, laundries and ice-cream machines; air-conditioned living and working spaces. Jack, while affecting to mock these 'luxuries', envied them. True, his Yankee opposite number did not enjoy Jack's daily tot of rum, but even that time-hallowed perquisite, did Jack but know it, was coming under the baleful scrutiny of atomic-age admirals, united in regarding rum as 'the curse of the Navy in the second half of the twentieth century'.[1]

The Admiralty, amid all its other preoccupations, was obliged to give consideration to these expectations, and many were the well-intentioned committees set up in Whitehall. In the way of committees, concrete results were a long time coming. A former First Sea Lord and Chief of Defence Staff was to write: 'It seems inconceivable that long overdue reforms in conditions of service should have taken so long to set in motion . . . married quarters, tolerable living conditions ashore and afloat, and many other amenities properly taken for granted by the other two Services, took many years to become a reality. . . .'[2] This is not hypocrisy from a head of the Navy who was too junior at the time in question to bear much blame for that state of affairs. An improved pay code, at least, was introduced in 1946, but that was easily done.

In all new constructions, and in such ships as were undergoing major reconstruction, many new and improved amenities were being included. But there was little scope (as distinct from room!) for improvement in the older warships retained in service out of economic and political necessity, because of the need to accommodate a mass of new technological equipment such as advanced radar, communications systems and electronic weaponry. Since the days of the Dreadnoughts, more space for gizmos had meant less for sailors.

The first postwar decade was a time of retrenchment and great upheaval for the Royal Navy with disposal of surplus ships, demobilization of Hostilities-Only and time-expired regular personnel, and problems in manning those ships remaining – the minimum considered necessary to meet Britain's overseas commitments at a time when delusions of Empire still clouded the nation's collective vision. The Admiralty had much on its plate, not least the new Labour government's demand that the Navy democratize its officer selection and entry system, and it is perhaps understandable if the lower deck (rarely, it must be said, at the very core of the Admiralty's concerns; at least, not since Invergordon) should be left behind in the race for modernization. But the problem of recruitment and retention was central to all else, and would have to be addressed.[3]

Senior naval officers of the period, in their memoirs and reminiscences, sometimes betray the officer caste's – how shall we put it? – not indifference, exactly: inadvertency, perhaps, about postwar expectations, aspirations and motivation generally on the lower deck. This is not surprising in view of their Dartmouth-stamp education and training, little changed from the Edwardian era, combined with the Royal Navy's notorious conservatism and devotion to tradition; much more marked than among the officer classes of the British Army and Royal Air Force. As one naval officer, by no means the most blinkered of his kind, or even among the top hundred, somewhat plaintively observed, 'There was not really the same professionalism and cohesion in the lower-deck class as there had been before . . .',[4] which does rather beg the question if by 'before' he meant, as he probably did, 'before the war'. The 1930s able seaman with his thirty shillings (£1.50) a week and all found was content enough, with all his hardships, when the certain alternative was unemployment, means test and dole. This was not the case postwar, quite the contrary, with full employment in most parts of the country and high wages for even unskilled labour. Sailors' pay, notwithstanding the 1946 increase, fell far short of 'outside' rates and there was no compensation, as there is today with the 'X-factor', for domestic disruption and for generally being at one's country's call.

Wives had changed too, and were less inclined than their mothers had been to accept the lengthy separations that were still the lot of the Navy wife. For almost the whole of the postwar decade (in fact until July 1954, when they were reduced by a year) foreign service commissions were still of two and a half years' duration (more on some stations), unchanged since before the First World War. Again, the admirals would have kept it so. It was their firm belief that a shorter commission did not get full value from a well shaken-down and cohesive ship's company, and was therefore to the detriment of the service. But much more detrimental was the increasing reluctance of senior rates coming to the end of their 12-year engagements to sign on for pension – men the service could ill-afford to lose.

The contrasting attitudes of the wardroom and the lower deck to things as they were in those years are illustrated in the following passages. First, Capt. P.W. Brock, DSO, RN, in his valedictory message on relinquishing command of HMS *Kenya* on the Far East station in June 1951:

The opportunities we have had of seeing some of the fine ships of the United States Navy, must, at times, have given rise to feelings of envy of their modern design and equipment with its profusion of weapons, labour-saving devices and domestic comforts. [A little defensive in tone perhaps, but then the true voice of the British naval officer:] It need not, however, give rise to an inferiority complex. There are at least two equally important factors on which we have no reason to fear comparison. One is the human factor; another is tradition.

Then a Seaman Torpedoman of that era, John Crew:

It was not until, I should say, 1946 that those of us still around could pause to reflect and survey our present situation. . . . It was agreed by the Admiralty that pre-war conditions, discipline etc, would be restored as soon as possible. The decree was quickly abandoned – but it had done damage! Something was very wrong with that organization. I left the service in March 1956. I had been lied to for nearly all my service – about new short foreign service commissions, better living conditions, food, uniform and so on. There were *four* married quarters for 21,000 men in Chatham Division the day I left!

Slowly, change came. Some years after my own service, in the pursuance of a different duty, I found myself below decks in one of the first new class of guided missile cruisers. How spacious it all seemed – roomy, well-lit flats and alley-ways, their decks a housewife's dream of polished, polychrome plastic tiling. Stainless steel was abundant, not least in the spotless, gleaming, all-electric galley; a bright and welcoming junior rates' cafeteria in steel and formica with curtains at the scuttles, messdecks the same, with folding bunks and not a hammock-bar in sight! It all smelled better, too.

This transformation together with many other, quite radical, changes for the better in conditions of service ashore and afloat, had finally come about by the early 1960s. Since then, the modern Royal Navy has progressed by leaps and bounds, as if intent on making up for a century of brassbound conservatism. Perhaps too far and too fast, for some. For Jack himself is conservative – none more so – and of the old sailors who relate their experiences of a vanished navy in the pages of this book; men who prided themselves on the cleanliness of their persons and their surroundings, on their domestic skills and making the best of what they were given – few would have reflected, as they 'scrubbed out' for Captain's rounds, peeled spuds and mixed flour and lard for a 'clacker', that there were more useful ways for a highly-trained serviceman to be spending his time.

What follows is the authentic voice of the lower deck; recollecting, not always in tranquillity, the atmosphere of a particular milieu at a particular time in a service never well known to the public at large, who despite that (or perhaps because of it) had a soft spot for Jack. My respondents, elderly men by definition, have their own views and perceptions of a period of their lives which left its ineradicable mark on their lifetime character and outlook. I have not presumed to edit except, occasionally, in the interests of clarity – this is how it was . . .

CHAPTER ONE

Lash Up And Stow!

The living-space below decks in a Royal Navy warship in which a junior rating (leading hand and below) of the 1940s and '50s ate, slept and had his being, was known as a broadside mess. In its essentials, this living-space had changed little since Nelson's sailors had eaten their victuals and slung their hammocks in little groups on the gundeck between a pair of broadside guns; hence the name. This surprising assertion bears repeating: one hundred and fifty years on, had a Jack tar of HMS *Foudroyant* or *Temeraire* been miraculously rematerialized on a mid-twentieth-century warship's messdeck, he would have recognized his surroundings at once and, reassured, made himself at home.

It is necessary for the reader to appreciate this fact in order to comprehend the philosophical acceptance and toleration of his situation on the part of the postwar rating – albeit, it must be said, not without a good deal of 'dripping', the matelot's prerogative down the ages. But even he was becoming aware that he deserved something better, as some ex-ratings testify below. It was dangerous for officers to persist in their assumption that Jolly Jack's sole preoccupations remained the famous 'Three Ps' of Pay, Prick and Pud. This assumption, like much else in the wardroom attitude to the lower deck, was out of date.

As will be seen from the accounts which follow, overcrowding was a common experience in both large and small ships. I lived for a year on an aircraft-carrier's messdeck which measured some 80 feet by 40 feet and accommodated 150 ratings. Known as the 'Snake Pit', it was located deep in the ship below the water-line, was inadequately ventilated, particularly in foul weather, and TB was endemic. This, the ship's Principal Medical Officer solemnly warned us, was due to our draping freshly-laundered underwear on the hammock bars to dry. His medical colleagues may have been as surprised as we were to learn that the White Plague was caused by damp Y-fronts.

The Snake Pit was the main seamen's messdeck, but the naval airman junior rates were hardly better off:

My mess was Air maintenance Deck 9. This was the home for all flight personnel below the rank of petty officer. It consisted of a compartment with one watertight door, 3 Port Holes and 5 tables numbered 3, 5, 7, 9, 11. Ratings living here were Pilots' Mates, Engine Ratings, Airframe Ratings, Armament Ratings. AMD9 Table was about 10ft long 2ft 6in wide and served on average about 16 people, to eat off it and live on it. When squadrons came on board more were allocated to mess and this often needed three sittings for meals.

The sleeping places were above table and walkway with hammock slinging for about 8 people in hammocks, the remainder slung their hammocks in the passage way outside the mess and onto the weather-deck which was open to the elements. The hammock had a very thin mattress, no pillow – usually the clothes you took off were rolled up and used as a pillow, also one blanket.

When I joined the ship my slinging space was on weather deck and as people left you moved to the passage and eventually to a position above mess table . . . toilets were about 4 decks down and washplace amidships, also for washing and ironing your own clothes.

(D. Harding, Leading Electrician, HMS *Illustrious* 1949–50)

A messmate of LEM Harding has recollections from the same period:

Our messdeck was situated right up for'ard on the starboard side, with the anchor dangling right outside – and didn't we know it when we were in rough weather . . . our messdeck comprised of some five mess tables each one having at least a dozen blokes on it and of course hammocks – no bunks! . . . One thing you quickly learn to accept is the ability to get on with your messmates, learning to accept the local home-made rules for Uckers[1] and numerous other games, learning to share fairly when it came to food being dished out, to say nothing of the all-important tot-time! Also of great importance was learning to accept that when hammocks went up, it was sardine time – they were so tightly positioned it was unbelievable – but you soon got to accept it even though it got more than a bit hairy in rough weather.

(L. Mossop, Leading Radio Mechanic, HMS *Illustrious* 1949–50)

In such intimate proximity one got to know one's messmates very well, as may be imagined. Personal mannerisms were, perforce, tolerated within reason; personal odours were not, hence the matelot's almost obsessive cleanliness of body and clothing. And lest the word 'intimate' be misconstrued, it should be noted that homosexuality, contrary to legend, was all but unknown on the lower deck.

. . . your mention of the cramped conditions prompted a recollection which may interest you (I guess it's part recollection and part social observation really). During my time on board it wasn't unusual, for those of us who had the opportunity, to seek out hidey-holes in which to escape from crowded messdecks. My oppo Don Norman and I had such a hidey-hole in the shape of the Air Radio Storeroom, located somewhere in the bowels. We found this a great place to sling our hammocks and enjoy a quiet read, and we shared it for several months . . .

[The social observation bit would seem to be as follows:] in those more innocent days, our disappearance from the messdeck every evening at 'Pipe Down' gave no rise to ribald comment whatsoever. Nor did it for any of the other lads who went off to sleep elsewhere (I hasten to add that we were all enthusiastically trying to become practising heterosexuals). I doubt if two blokes could have similar sleeping arrangements today without being accused of being something that we certainly were not!

In fact, despite some well-worn jokes about what are now known as 'gays', and a persistent rumour about some steward or other, my recollection is that any activities of that sort were either non-existent or exceptionally well concealed. I do recall a three-badge[2] Leading Torpedoman called 'Badges' something, who used to put the fear of God into trainee Naval Airmen by accosting them on their way back from the showers with remarks like '*You* smell nice, sunshine' – but 'Badges' was married with three or four kids and an unorthodox sense of humour.

(L. Dennis, Leading Radio Mechanic, HMS *Illustrious* 1948–9)

To continue a little further down this sidetrack: despite the foregoing, it was not unknown for a sailor with a taste for high living beyond the reach of his meagre pay to allow himself to be entertained ashore by wealthy homosexuals, both in home and foreign ports. This meretricious practice was known as 'baron-strangling', and was admired rather than condemned by the strangler's messmates.

Also, in what was essentially a monastic society, good-looking boys and young seamen (referred to as 'skin'), though rarely in any real danger, undoubtedly stirred from time to time – usually at tot-time – whatever latent leanings existed within a ship's company. It is not immodest of me (who barely qualified), to recall an occasion when, encountering in a narrow alley-way a burly and very hairy chief telegraphist clad only in a towel, I was startled to be seized in a bear-hug and subjected to a wet kiss. Following which both parties went about their business; the incident, if not forgotten, was never subsequently referred to, or repeated.

To return to the messdeck . . .

Every mess had, fixed to the bulkhead, an open-fronted aluminium locker with spaces to store plates, mugs, a few bottles etc. and with drawers in which to store the 'eating-irons' – knives, forks, spoons and the like. There was also, below this locker and secured by a quickly-detachable fitting of lugs and drop-in pins, a long wooden table, flanked on each side by long wooden benches or 'stools' with drop-down securable metal legs. Stowed at the ship's-side end of the table beneath the mess-trap locker was a large, rectangular metal box, complete with lid and a central handle. This was divided internally into two halves; one for tea (loose leaves, no tea-bags then!) and the other for sugar. Milk was more of a problem because we were virtually confined to tinned milk; both the gooey, over-sweet 'condensed' and the thinner but less-loved by most, 'evaporated' varieties. Condensed was much scarcer and certainly less economical than evaporated, so the latter was the most-used.

One item of equipment I have not mentioned, kept in every mess in the big locker, was a large, round, much-scarred bread board. No sliced bread, as we know the accursed stuff today, then existed – unless, that is, 'Chef' could be persuaded to 'run it through yer slicer'. We got our loaves, all tin loaves as a rule, to be sliced as required.

Another essential of every mess was the large galvanized 'gash bucket' that stood below table-level at the other (inboard) end of the mess. This was for the sole purpose of holding all the table-refuse for disposal after every meal. At sea the contents would be ditched via the 'gash-chutes' which were fixed to the ship's side so that the swill could be shot over into the sea. In harbour alongside, it would be carried ashore for disposal in a pound. A gash bucket had to be kept as clean as possible, for reasons of hygiene in such crowded conditions. It fell to the duty 'cook of the mess' appointed on a rota basis, to do so. It was often a very disagreeable task – and many just could not cope with the greasy, gummy, smelly contents; even when tied-up alongside and not feeling queasy.

Also not mentioned was the 'tea-fanny' – nothing like Mum's decorated bone china, nor like the big, brown enamelled teapot beloved of so many kitchens and canteens. This was a large tall aluminium 'pot' which had no 'pot' – it just went all the way up at the same width to a small lid in the centre of the flat top of the can which gave access to a long, perforated tube-like 'infuser' which extended nearly to the bottom. It had a wide, swing-up handle and a spout to the side. This was filled, almost to the top, with steam-heated water from one of the galley's many points and a few handfuls (God bless all the rationed civilians) of dry tea leaves in the central infuser and left to 'mash' – and a damned good brew could be had in this way.

(M. Bree, Leading Writer, HMS *Woolwich* 1949)

Standards of messdeck hygiene, for which leading hands of messes were held accountable, were checked and monitored daily at evening 'rounds' by the officer of the day (in harbour) or the officer of the watch (at sea). The ultimate, most minute and searching inspection, however, was the hallowed Naval institution of 'Captain's Rounds', which took place every Saturday forenoon, ashore and afloat, throughout the Navy.

All these aluminium utensils were at least hygienic – they could also be well burnished with 'Bluebell' for Captain's Rounds on Saturday morning. Everything about the 'Andrew'[3] was founded on tradition, and that applied to the method of laying out mess-traps for inspection in traditional patterns. The tea chest, mess kettle and bread board had to be laid centrally near the end of the table, with knives, forks and spoons arrayed precisely round the latter's circumference (see Plate 1). Every last part of the mess-deck, bulkheads, table; our kit-lockers, inside and out – had to be spotless and squared-off for the eagle-eyed inspection. There were, too, those officers who took a perverse delight in poking white-gloved fingers into the most obscure nooks and crannies in order to have something to fault and someone to blame. Usually the leading hand.

(M. Bree, Leading Writer, HMS *Woolwich* 1949)

The RN always designed a warship then put the people in where ever they could fit them, this of course left all accommodation higgledy-piggledy. I remember our mess on *Dido* was bent around 'A' barbette[4] and as it was in the days of portholes (18-inch if I remember rightly) it was probably the best natural lighting I ever lived in at sea.

(R. Jamieson, Boy Seaman, HMS *Dido* 1946)

And it had probably the best ventilation. Mention has been previously made of the prevalence of tuberculosis on the lower deck, considerably higher than was now the case ashore. A friend of Boy Jamieson's succumbed: '. . . he was discharged with TB late in 1949 and I remember visiting him in his little hut with sides they could hoist up, at Ulverston I think. I remember him lying there with open sides to the hut in a temperature of about 40°F, saying it was great as he was getting a pint of stout a day free of cost. Such was the stoicism of boy seamen RN'.

Boy Jamieson later transferred to the Royal Australian Navy and ended his service as Chief Petty Officer Coxswain, skipper of a search and rescue launch at Jervis Bay. The RAN was not immune; in 1948 HMAS *Arunta* returned to Australia from the Far East with no less than a third of her ship's company stricken with TB. This was the worst incidence in RAN history, though it should be noted that *Arunta* was a British-designed Tribal class destroyer. Still, such a high incidence of shipboard disease can hardly have been seen in the tropics since the days of scurvy.

Unlike TB, which was an all too real and ever-present threat to the sailor's health, nothing was ever heard of asbestosis in ships whose very arteries were asbestos-lagged pipes snaking through messdecks and machinery spaces. Until my researches for this book revealed otherwise, I regarded asbestosis (except among workers in the industry) as a chimera in an era of Domesday health scares when an entire neighbourhood can be put on alert and schools closed upon discovery of asbestos in someone's loft. Of course such an exaggerated reaction is merely in keeping with the modern tendency to hysteria in health matters, but I now realize that the reason I had never heard of a case of asbestosis in the Navy, was that it was rarely diagnosed as such. There were many cases, however, particularly among the engineroom branch, and here is a typical example:

> I worked in the boiler room, engine-room and everything is covered in asbestos. In heavy seas and when the ship was firing her broadsides there would be clouds of asbestos dust and burnt-oil soot which after 7 years got to me and caused me to be invalided out with lung trouble, which 40 years later was diagnosed as Asbestosis caused by asbestos and hydrocarbon soot, when I received a pension of 80% which I should have received in 1954, for which quite a few of us are taking our case to the House of Lords and possibly the European Court of Justice.
>
> (D. Macfarlane, Stoker Mechanic, HMS *Ocean* 1954)

But healthy young sailors were careless of possible exposure to disease. They were aware of day-to-day discomforts and deprivations; aware, too, that they were not getting a fair deal, though it needs the perspective of passing years to voice their sense of injustice:

Arethusa, born in an era of deep depression amidst a welter of international treaty obligations, was severely restricted in design as a large destroyer.[5] Her build reflected the severe stratification of the deeply divided class society of the day. I always thought the opulence of the officers' quarters – the mahogany, the comfort, the galley, the pantry, the stewards, the wardroom and above all, the space – was far too disproportionate to the lower deck, hopelessly overcrowded and noisy. Movement on the messdeck was severely impeded by the three-foot coaming between the messes. There was total lack of any privacy, even in the 'heads'. The bathroom was primitive in the extreme – just pivoted enamel basins over a galvanized trough. One took a bath using only a bucket. One washed all over then threw the remaining water over oneself to rinse off. If lucky one had a second bucket of water – but no more.

(J. Crew, Seaman Torpedoman HMS *Arethusa* 1947)

Down our messdeck which was forward, we took a lot of stick in bad weather and often lost crockery which we had to pay for to replace. Our hammocks were so close that to get in your hammock when you came off watch, you would have to push several sleeping to make a gap big enough to pull yourself up and swing in.

For washing we had a bathroom (for about 24 of us) 7 feet square with 3 handbasins and one cold-water tap. Hot water was sometimes available from the galley opposite, if not it was hard cheese! The officers had a bathroom with a bath and each one had his own flunkey to cater for him, and of course they all had a handbasin in their cabins with hot and cold water.

We engine-room staff were lucky because we could 'borrow'(!) water from the main steam tanks (for the boilers) and it was always piping-hot. Also myself and another leading hand ran the 'dhobey firm'.[6] We washed the hammocks of all the crew, the captain fixing the tariff, on my stint it was 6 old pence (2½p) per hammock. We would dhobey them when off watch during the first watch (2000 to midnight) when there wasn't much demand for the bathroom.

(D. Banks, Leading Stoker Mechanic, HMS *Bleasdale* 1949)

Ratings were expected to keep their persons and their kit clean, with the most rudimentary facilities for bathing and laundering. Men in square rig,[7] routinely inspected at Sunday Divisions and before going ashore on liberty or duty, were required to turn out in Number One uniform pressed in the regulation fashion, i.e. with three vertical creases to the blue jean collar and six 'athwartship' creases in their bell-bottoms.

Characteristically, no irons were officially provided, and so another opportunity was created for the messdeck entrepreneur.

> Regarding cleanliness on board any vessel, it was in the main generally accepted that nearly all personnel kept themselves clean, usually by a daily shower, which incorporated a sort of washing session (called 'dhobeying') during which the 'smalls' of individuals were washed in a bucket, wrung-out and, with the consent of the Engineering Dept, strung out in the upper reaches of the boiler room allocated for this purpose. On large ships, i.e. cruisers, battleships, carriers, depot ships – laundries were provided, staffed by Chinese ratings, and very good they were too. For this service, the ratings had to pay nominal sums. But with the items returned spotless and ironed, ready to wear, the advent of aboard-ship laundries was a wonderful boon. Not so with small ships.
>
> Ratings would collect their 'dhobeying' from wheresoever they'd chosen to dry, and then came an often vexing and frustrating performance of ironing. The wherewithal to iron one's clothes for Divisions, or runs ashore, consisted usually of persuading one member of the mess to 'Lend us yer iron, mate!' It was an item not issued by their Lordships, and so was left to the foresight and mercenary endeavours of a few ratings who'd usually purchased one from shore-wards or the NAAFI stores. Always in great demand, especially just before the advent of long leave, the owners made a bomb. Many a week's tot (rum issue) was quite blatantly sacrificed by those desirous of looking 'tiddley' (very smart) if they had a burning-date ashore etc., and often money changed hands.
>
> (F. Woods, Leading Stoker, HMS *Contest* 1951)

One wonders about the 'nearly all' above. It might hint at the drastic but salutory cure, traditionally applied to a messmate who was less than meticulous in his daily ablutions; a rare creature indeed and known as a 'crabby skate'. Such a defaulter was in breach of Jack's holiest canon, and should he persist in his antisocial ways after due warning, he was hauled off to the washroom, forcibly stripped, doused with cold water and given a brisk scrubbing with long-handled deck scrubbers. A second dose of the cure was unknown. The wardroom would know nothing of this: it took for granted, as it took so much of the lower deck for granted, that Jack's turn-out would at all times be a credit to his ship and the service; his pride and self-respect, presumably, surmounting such trifling obstacles as a lack of the most basic on-board amenities.

Another *rara avis* on the lower deck, though for a quite different reason, was one such as the next contributor, an Old Etonian, and a natural member of the officer-caste temporarily out of his natural element. Junior ratings of a similar background and nurture were not uncommon during the war years, when their adaptability and talent for earning the respect of their shipmates was a cause of admiration and a credit to the public school ethos. Writer Whiteley's account is included here because he was among the last of the Hostilities-Only ratings to be conscripted under wartime regulations, just before the first peacetime national servicemen appeared, bringing a fresh sprinkling of public-school boys to the messdecks. After initial training, he was drafted to a six-inch cruiser in dry dock at Portsmouth:

As the ship was in dry dock for an extensive refit, it was overrun with workmen, power and compressed air cables, dirt and deafening drilling noises. The ship did not have a full complement and, apart from myself and a Chief Writer, the only other member of the Supply and Secretariat branch were two Stores Assistants. Us junior rates shared a small broadside mess with about 8 seamen and conditions were far from pleasant. We all slept where we could – several of the hammock hooks were unavailable due to them being used to carry loose thick cables – and I bedded down on one of the side benches. The heads were, of course, out of action as were the ablution areas. We had to use the dockside facilities, showers (I will concede that the water was always hot) and latrines built in the 19th century (a row of bum-holes and torn newspaper). At night, for bladder relief only, we used an old rum fanny in the mess and it was usually my task, as the youngest and most junior, to empty it!

Whenever I could afford it – it cost a shilling (5p) – I slept ashore in one of the hostels, and so did many of the others. Evening shore-leave was generous, it needed to be, and apart from those on watch most of us went ashore after the workmen had gone. As for myself, my runs ashore generally started late, as I was confined in the Captain's Office struggling to type word-perfect letters to their Lordships. I had never been faced with a typewriter before – believe it or not, my Writer's training syllabus did not include typing – so it was a time-consuming struggle.

(J.M. Huntington-Whiteley, Writer, HMS *Glasgow* 1948)

This writer identifies with the early-morning struggle ashore with a brimming piss-bucket, as that task often fell to him during the six-week docking of an aircraft-carrier at Devonport. Unlike the *Glasgow*, most of

HMS *Glasgow*

the ship's company lived aboard throughout the refit, so the aforesaid receptacle contained the nocturnal easings of some 200 bladders in the forward crew accommodation. The huge pail held several gallons, but was always half a gallon less than the capacity needed. It was carried ashore, a broomstick through the handle of the pail, by two duty hands taking short, careful steps along numerous alley-ways, companionways and down the gangplank, any crewman encountered en route ducking for cover.

If living aboard a warship in commission could be rated uncomfortable, living aboard during a refit was purgatory. The ship was taken over by hordes of 'fearnought'-clad dockyard 'maties', who with their welding machines, pneumatic hammers, snaking fathoms of power and air lines and their less than dainty habits quickly reduced Jack's immaculate environment to a dirty, littered, smelly, clamorous hell's kitchen. Only the dear Lord and the Admiral Superintendent knew why most of the crew could not be landed to the vast, half-empty RN barracks a few hundred yards from the ship, as most of the officers were. There may have been a good and adequate reason which was not vouchsafed to sailors.

Jack's adaptability knew no bounds:

During a two-and-a-half year commission on the Far East station I served on a frigate from 1951 to 1953. This was during the Korean War. With a wartime complement aboard the living quarters were packed. As a Telegraphist I lived in the Communications Mess, starboard side, forward. The mess consisted of one long table about

14

ten feet long, cushioned lockers down one side and two wooden benches the other, provided seating. There were some upright lockers, some steel open lockers secured to one of the bulkheads containing eating utensils, and a hammock stowage. This was home for twenty-two men for the duration of the commission.

Normally at sea the ship would be in four watches but in wartime conditions this would change, becoming three watches. This in fact made things a little easier because instead of their being only a quarter of the mess away on duty at any one time, there was a third. More room in the mess. At action stations naturally each person would be at exactly that so the mess would be virtually empty.

It was often very difficult during shipboard life, not only to sleep in a hammock, but to find a place to actually sling one's hammock. It was very rarely the case that, e.g. with twenty mess members there would be twenty spaces to sling hammocks. Therefore, those without would have to find a space outside the mess. Maybe in gangways or passageways outside offices not always in use. Within these passageways etc., when the ship was at sea, the noise could be horrendous. This could of course become familiar ground and after a few days the noise seemed to become 'switched out' and you fell cosily asleep. Of course there was the opposite effect, e.g. one messmate slung his hammock right alongside an extremely noisy ventilation fan. He, after a few days, mentally switched out this noise and easily fell asleep. Until one night when the fan broke down and stopped completely. He immediately woke shouting, 'What's that? What's that?'

(J. Leach, Telegraphist, HMS *Mounts Bay* 1953)

Another flash of recognition for me, when I moved my kitbag and hammock forward to a seamen's messdeck on rating up from Boy in 1948. For the junior member, the hammock billet allocated was directly above a piece of machinery called a hull and fire pump. Its function was to maintain pressure in the ship's fire main, and it would switch in, and out, at fitful, unpredictable intervals with a high-pitched whine. This was not, be it noted, in an outside alley-way never meant for sleeping quarters but plumb bang in the middle of a sailors' messdeck, placed there by an unthinking, malign or incompetent naval constructor. Given the many other demands on Jack's adaptability and endurance, he might have been spared noisy machinery in his immediate environment.

Regarding health and fitness, Jack, being the versatile character he was, always seemed to have a remedy or antidote for any malady, from a hangover to deathbed flu. Of course, conditions on many ships did not lend themselves to a healthy environment, and packed together as they were, attempting to live and behave in a civilized manner was not easy. On my own deck, 6 and 7 Messes consisted of some 34 to 38 Stokers attempting to relax after a long watch, or write home, read, make and mend, clean to go ashore; even a temporarily-sick Stoker in his hammock; the air thick and foul-smelling with cigarette smoke, men's sweating bodies, etc. At sea it is even worse. All scuttles (portholes) are firmly closed and the only circulation of air comes from a draught-fan system which never was adequate. So you can imagine how it felt to be 'down below' at sea, and often in harbour.

So Jack used to take himself up top when he was off-watch at sea and, weather permitting, would cover the whole of the upper deck in a steady stroll, usually with an 'oppo', and there would be quite a number of these pairs on the upper deck, especially towards sunset, of all ranks and ratings. A half-hour or even an hour of this exercise was the norm for the majority of shipbound crews, and the exercise proved beneficial. On big ships such as carriers and battlewagons organized parties doubled round the flight deck or gun platforms under the PTI.

(F. Woods, Leading Stoker, HMS *Contest* 1951)

Ratings would not normally 'cover the whole of the upper deck' on their dogwatch promenades, as the usual demarcations applied in allocation of deck space as in other matters. On a small ship such as a destroyer or frigate, for instance, junior ratings were usually confined to the quarterdeck, the more spacious forecastle being reserved for the officers and chief and petty officers: starboard side for the officers, chiefs and POs to port. On big ships – cruisers and above – the snowy-scrubbed quarterdeck was hallowed ground, trodden only by commissioned feet.

Jack's main bogey at sea seemed to be the dreaded flu-bug. He would accept and weather all kinds of tropical maladies, and bumps and bruises and still do a full watch, but the flu knocked him for six. For some unaccountable reason, the medical branch did not look upon flu as anything but a bad cold, and 'medicine and duty' was invariably prescribed by the docs. So, he was obliged to do what he could on board or in barracks to cure himself. Hence the occasionally slung hammock on board, or the recumbent 'body' ashore. One found one's messmates very loyal in their endeavours to 'cover up' for each other in all respects. The 'strokes' that were pulled were unbelievable at times, but they always worked!

As opposed to today's Navy, sea-sickness was not even considered to be any sort of malady which might enable a rating to forgo a watch, duty, or attendance when required. There were extreme cases, rare, and these were usually dealt with ashore, the rating concerned usually advised of his suitability to continue in the service. You may not think so, but it was a very serious matter for a rating to be 'Discharged: Unsuitable for Sea Service,' and no wounds, missing limbs, or medals to show for it. Just, 'I was always sea-sick, sir' at a job interview or idle curiosity at his local pub. Although he couldn't be blamed, his dignity and self-respect were injured internally. I know. I met one or two.

So, if he was indisposed, he did his best to 'grin and bear it' so to speak, hoping to be drafted to a shore-base, or a big ship which didn't bounce about all over the water as in, say, a destroyer, frigate, escort or similar. Most of us coped. Some, just.'

(F. Woods, Leading Stoker, HMS *Contest* 1951)

Every British warship in commission, without exception, was infested with cockroaches. Routine fumigation had no lasting effect and it must have been the general ambience of an HM ship, as of the kitchens of expensive restaurants (so, maybe, the luxury food served in the wardroom) which caused them to thrive. Air-pressure variations and a whiff of battery-gas did not inconvenience them, for they were particularly numerous in submarines. They were very fond of ground coffee, one of the 'extras' issued to submarine crews. On a boat in which I served, an effective cockroach trap was to wedge an empty coffe tin with a few grains of bean left at the bottom, among the overhead pipes. The eager insects would hurl themselves recklessly in, landing with a faint *ping*, and would of course be unable to climb out again after the feast. When alongside or in 'silent running' mode submerged, with machinery stilled, it was possible by placing one's ear close to the tin to hear the tiny but powerful jaws crunching their last meal.

The ship rats referred to in the following account were a rarity in home waters; much commoner in foreign ports and particularly in the tropics:

Wild Goose was lying in Walker's Yard at Colombo undergoing a short refit before sailing to the Gulf. We were housed in the British Sailors' and Soldiers' Institute until the work was completed.

A week before sailing all the ship's hatches were sealed off. Before the last hatch was shut a team of local Singalese activated smoke bombs and other types of rodent repellent, then closed the hatch.

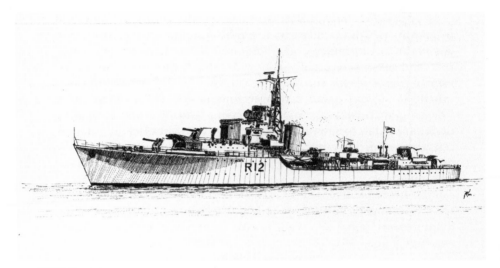

HMS *Contest*

After 3 days the hatches were opened and the job of clearing out the dead rats and cockroaches began. I forget how many oil-drumsful we ended up with. A few days after entering the Indian Ocean rats that had died in the ventilation shafts began to make their presence felt. We had to use wire hooks attached to poles to try and retrieve the corpses.

(R. Anderson, Able Seaman, HMS *Wild Goose* 1953)

The *Black Swan* class were probably the most heavily-armed frigates in the world at that time. They had three 4.5 inch turrets, a 'Hedgehog' anti-submarine mortar with 24 spigots on each of which was a 64 lb bomb and on the quarterdeck, depth charges on both port and starboard sides and aft. And of course, two Bofors AA guns. I've forgotten the number of men which made up the ship's company but we were very overcrowded. There were no bunks then – we all had hammocks but there wasn't enough hammock space for all, so we slept on the benches round the mess table. When the weather permitted some of us slept on the upper deck, until it rained in the middle of the night when we would bed-down in the passageways. We'd take a can of beer to sip in the night. Sometimes it tasted 'lumpy' – cockroaches used to get in.

(A. Zammit, Ordinary Seaman, HMS *Modeste* 1955)

Men can accustom themselves to almost anything in time, and 'custom reconciles'. An outsider's reaction can then startle, and it is an outsider's reaction which ends this chapter:

We returned to the UK in 1949 after 2 years and 8 months in the Med. My parents came down to Chatham to meet the ship on our arrival home to pay off and I remember after the tour of the ship finishing up on the messdeck my mother, who did not cry easily, wept uncontrollably when she finally became aware of how and where we lived on board. She never again expressed desire to see any other ship.

(G. Jay, Able Seaman, HMS *Phoebe* 1949)

CHAPTER TWO

Cooks to the Galley!

In 1750, sailors in men-of-war were issued with raw victuals which, when they required it, were prepared for cooking by the recipients themselves before delivery to the ship's cook. In 1950, except in shore establishments and big ships, sailors were issued with raw victuals which they prepared themselves and took to the galley for cooking. This single fact probably illustrates better than any other the extraordinary conservatism, or hidebound customs, of the Royal Navy; a mind-set pickled in brine.

In the modern age with which we are concerned, this system of messing was known as 'canteen messing'. Under this arrangement provisions such as meat, fresh vegetables, flour, margarine, sugar and tea were issued gratis to individual messes from ship's stores, in the quantities laid down according to the number of men victualled in each mess. In addition, a small per capita allowance was made for the purchase of such 'luxuries' as eggs, pickles, tinned beans and so forth from the ship's canteen; hence the name. Food preparation was done by 'cooks of messes'; that is, by mess-members in turn, usually teamed in pairs and usually on cook duties for 24 hours at a time.

A large part of this duty was the preparation of the mess's dinner, eaten at midday. What the meal comprised was determined largely by the cut of meat issued to the mess on any given day by the ship's 'tanky' or amateur butcher. When this was a joint of beef or pork, the cook's task was easy; the meat was trimmed and placed in a baking tin tallied with the mess number. Peeled potatoes were arranged round the joint which was conveyed to the galley, usually with a second vegetable such as cabbage in a separate tallied utensil. This dish was known as 'schooner on the rocks', or 'a straight rush'.

Having enjoyed a joint of meat one day, it was likely that a mess's next ration would be stewing meat or scrag-end ('the bullock took a pace step-back, an' we got a slice off the 'orns'). This would be cut up, supplemented with carrots and onions, and often with leaden dumplings known as 'depth-charges' to make a 'pot-mess'. If he felt equal to it the duty cook might essay a pie crust, or 'clacker' with meat and potatoes beneath. Whatever was produced, it will be readily understood that the quality of the meal depended much upon the experience and aptitude, or the lack of them, of the seaman, stoker or electrician's mate who found himself cook for a day.

The system itself was wasteful, involving as it did the piecemeal issue and preparation of food. It was also open to abuse, for the per capita allowance was credited monthly to the mess caterer or leading hand and at the end of a month any 'mess savings' were paid over to him to be shared out. Senior hands of messes were sometimes more interested in beer money than in solid sustenance; where such was the case, ill-feeling could arise when younger, hungrier members saw a neighbouring mess feeding better than they were. Furthermore, it was wasteful of trained mens' time at a period of manpower shortage. An hour or so after turning-to in the morning a duty cook would have to be released by his leading hand or petty officer in order to go below to prepare his messmates' dinner and deliver it to the galley by the PO cook's deadline. Above all, it was outdated, archaic, primitive and any other word to be found in a thesaurus.

The fact that canteen messing was tolerated for so long with so little to commend it – it survived in small ships such as destroyers and frigates until the late 1950s – speaks volumes for the Navy's ingrained sense of tradition. 'That's the way it's always been done'; older sailors, conservative as ever, disliked change and the wardroom had no interest. Such ad hoc messing was to persist in one form or another until the new ships of the postwar building programme joined the Fleet, properly designed and efficient; as much in crew accommodation and facilities as in weapons systems and electronics.

> The senior Leading Hand controlled the mess and his mess job was cleanliness, also checked once a day by duty officer and once a week by Captain or Commander. He would make a roster for 2 cooks to be on duty for 1 week at a time, their job was to collect food from the galley. Each rating had to peel and clean his own portion of vegetables. Items like butter were divided by the leading hand to prevent arguments. The food was taken to the galley, checked by chief cook for cleanliness and if OK, cooked, collected at meal time and served. The cooks would wash up, scrub table and benches, sweep deck and then go to service aircraft.
>
> (D. Harding, Leading Electrician, HMS *Illustrious* 1949–50)

As a detailed description of the canteen messing system and how it was operated, the following account could hardly be bettered. It includes the essential rum issue, a much-prized numbing agent to accompany an often unappetizing or inadequate dinner.

In small ship messes a system known as 'canteen messing' prevailed. It worked like this. Each month, messes were allocated a certain allowance to feed the occupants. The senior rating, usually a leading hand of some years experience, sorted out how much daily the mess could afford to spend on meals, replacement of crockery, utensils, and appliances appertaining to preparing, cooking and dishing up, and each day would detail two hands of the mess to act as 'cooks'. These two had the task of conjuring up the main meal of the day, usually dinner, and as you can imagine, many varieties of culinary art were performed accordingly, and taken up to the galley to be finalized by the Chief Cook and/or his mate. At around 1145 hours the pipes 'Cooks to the galley' and 'One hand from each mess muster for rum' were heard throughout the ship, The two ratings who were mess cooks for the day left their workplaces early and repaired to the galley. From here they collected the meal they had previously prepared, and took it below. On the messdeck, they spread the oilcloth on the table, assembled the appropriate number of plates, knives, forks etc. and doled out the prepared and cooked meal accordingly, during which time the hands would have assembled below in anticipation.

The leading hand usually took on himself the job of collecting the rum issue from the place where it was stored and guarded, usually the tiller flat (steering mechanism compartment). Upon attaining the age of 20 years each rating was allocated an issue of rum, usually diluted by two parts water to one part neat rum, and called two-plus-one, or 'plussers', each day at noon, and it was a much-prized 'drop of cheer' to many. Ratings lined up at the head of mess tables to receive their ration from the leading hand who, by courtesy and tradition, was always offered a small sip of his tot (called 'sippers') by each man. This fiery liquid, although reduced from its original neat strength by the addition of water, was invariably a welcome starter to the main meal.

When dinner-time was over and the hands returned to work, the two cooks of the mess cleaned up all round, washed up all utensils and gear and stowed them away, and swept the deck. They then reported this done to the leading hand, and that worthy usually inspected their work, and often made them do it again, depending on how he felt. The two men also cleaned up after tea, and just before 'Rounds' at 2100 hours. And that was it. A canteen messing ship.

(F. Woods, Leading Stoker, HMS *Contest*, Mediterranean 1951)

As a time-wasting, inefficient and cost-ineffective method of feeding a body of men, the canteen messing system might have been purposely designed to cause the maximum inconvenience, disruption and discontent among a ship's company. But it was not so designed, of course; it simply evolved down the ages like much else in the Royal Navy, aided by the sailor's own conservatism and his officers' indifference.

Conditions on the ship were the worst I encountered in the 13 years I was in the RN. We were what was known as 'broadside' or canteen messing. That meant an allowance of 6 shillings (30p) per head was allocated to each mess member for food for 24 hours. We had to elect a treasurer and a caterer; our mess, the quarterdeck mess, had around 24 members. The caterer made out a menu, all we could afford was a main meal at dinner-time and a meal at 1800. If you wanted anything for breakfast you bought it out of your own pocket from the canteen and cooked it yourself. We had to take it in turns to prepare the meal, i.e. peel the spuds, make the Yorkshire in an aluminum jug, also the gravy etc. and take it to the galley. We had Goanese cooks.

Bread was rationed, and it was also full of weevils. When you cut a slice it looked as though it had strawberry jam on, where the weevils had popped while being cooked. You soon learned to disregard them. Of course there weren't any fridges aboard in those days and food soon went off. We only ever had tinned milk and most of the veg. was dehydrated or tinned. Cockroaches were everywhere and whatever you did you couldn't get rid of them. The rats soon grew in numbers again and it wasn't uncommon to wake up to find one in your hammock.

The butcher used to give you the meat ration each day, you didn't have a choice, and when you took it to the galley in your tray (each mess had a brass tally with the mess number on) and you put your potatoes in a net bag with a wooden tally. If you got to the galley before another mess you would try and swap the joints of meat around for the larger one. This sometimes ended up in fist-fights. The only thing that kept you going was the daily tot of rum.

(R. Anderson, Able Seaman, HMS *Wild Goose*, Persian Gulf 1953)

This correspondent states, matter-of-factly and without comment, that 'of course' there were no refrigerators on board (I think he might have found one in the wardroom pantry). The *Bird* class of frigates, of which *Wild Goose* was one, were a wartime design, without frills and built as desperately-needed convoy escorts in the North Atlantic. Making every allowance for shortages of ships, men and money in the early 1950s, what does it say about the mentality and priorities of an Admiralty which could despatch a warship designed to operate in cold northern waters, ill-ventilated and packed with 200 men 'sweating their balls off', as they would graphically put it, afflicted with prickly-heat and other tropical maladies, to patrol one of the hottest places on earth without so much as a refrigerator to keep their food fresh?

Of course they would say they were doing their best in difficult circumstances. Here is a quotation from a naval history published in the mid-1970s, detailing the Royal Navy's transition to a nuclear age:[1]

> In all new construction ships and those refitting, efforts were begun to improve living conditions for ships' companies along lines which were already commonplace in the US Navy. Thus galley and bakery equipment was to be modernised, and facilities for bathing and washing clothes improved. The principle of separating recreational spaces from messes where men ate and slept was to be adopted as far as possible. Other amenities included the provision of automatic refrigerators, soda fountains and ice-cream machines, facilities for tailoring, boot repairing, dry cleaning and hairdressing. Labour-saving devices such as automatic chipping, scaling and paint-spraying machines would also be introduced ...
>
> But there were limitations to the extent of such improvements in older ships which were being retained, because of the need to accommodate the mass of new technical equipment such as radar and other electronic devices coming into service, higher speeds and better protection. These necessitated increased complements with consequent overcrowding of living spaces.

So there were improvements aplenty on the way, but they were an unconscionably long time coming. A subsequent chapter of the work quoted above is aptly titled 'Making Haste Slowly'; something the Admiralty excelled at.

The labour-saving devices mentioned above were hardly new. Compressed-air tools had been in use ashore in naval yards for many years, notably the 'windy hammers' deployed by dockyard maties in such clamorous numbers on ships in refit. But the simple 'dab-toe' sailor had only hand tools to perform his daily tasks. It was a common sight to see a flock of sailors hacking away at a vast bulkhead with chipping-hammers, like so many woodpeckers and with roughly the same effect, when a couple of pneumatic tools would have done the job in a tenth of the time. No doubt this was, to some extent, a manifestation of the 'make-work' factor mentioned in a later chapter. It seemed, too, that there always had to be a kind of penal servitude element in Jack's labours, as with convicts breaking rocks in Dartmoor quarries.

In any event, all this was a case of 'jam tomorrow'. Meantime, canteen messing still had years to run:

> We had 'canteen messing' which entailed the mess being credited with a few bob a day for each man in the mess. We all took turns to prepare the food which was taken to the galley. All the cook had to do was put the food in the oven or range. We (each mess) also had to do our own washing-up. Each forenoon all the food was prepared by the chap whose turn it was – usually help was on hand to peel the spuds. Occasionally someone would forget to draw the meat ration so you'd have tatties and veg for dinner. A favourite dessert was apple crumble made with dried apple-rings, this often had bits of steel-wire scourer in it as the trays hadn't been rinsed after washing.
>
> The thing with canteen messing was to have the ship's butcher or 'tanky' (who issued victualling stores) in your mess. Otherwise at the end of the month, everyone in the mess had to pay towards any overspending by the mess caterer. On the other hand, if the mess members were 'pizo' (mean) and ate frugally – you'd have a mess rebate to be shared among the members.
>
> (A. Zammit, Ordinary Seaman, HMS *Modeste* 1955)

The frequency with which cockroaches are mentioned in these accounts is an indication of their omnipresence on messdecks, in galleys and anywhere where food was stored or consumed. Jack learned to share his living space with them, but preferred not to include them in his diet:

> In most of my service days each mess did its own food. Each week two men would be known as mess cooks; they drew meat, fish, vegetables and other cooking stuff from the Paymaster's store. We prepared it ourselves according to what the majority of the mess wanted for that date. It was adequate but not brilliant, depending on who was doing the cooking. Except during the Korean war when we mostly lived on hard-tack biscuits, bread, corned beef and various tinned meats and fish. This would go on for weeks while you were at sea and only returned to normal when the ship came in to port for a boiler-clean or to change 6 in gun barrels which had worn out the rifling. In my case I used to spend quite a bit at the ship's NAAFI on things you didn't get in your normal diet. One of the nasty sides was the continual presence of cockroaches. When eating a meal you had to

hunch over the table covering your plate with your upper body, otherwise you could get cockroaches falling off the overhead trunking or pipes onto your plate or sandwiches, tea etc.

(D. Macfarlane, Stoker Mechanic, HMS *Ocean* 1950)

The alternative to canteen messing, introduced after the war in some bigger ships, was known as 'general messing'. Meals were still consumed on messdecks but were both prepared and cooked by trained cooks in the main galley, with a weekly menu ordained by the Supply Officer. General messing is described more fully below: the food was no better but the menu did include breakfast as a meal of sorts, rather than the canteen messing breakfast of 'a cup of tea and a walk round the mess table'. 'Cooks of messes' had merely to collect trays of food from the galley, dish it out and wash up afterwards:

We were required to take turns as duty mess cook and were responsible for getting the food for our own mess – down to the galley for a string bag of boiled spuds, together with a tray of whatever delight the chef had cooked up, back for another tray of duff, then down to the bakery flat to collect the bread. As long as you didn't worry too much about the cockroaches which seemed to delight in swarming all over the tops of the loaves – that was alright.

(L. Mossop, Leading Radio Mechanic, HMS *Illustrious* 1950)

After *Ganges* and *Indefatigable* I joined HMS *Montclare*, a converted 20,000-ton merchant ship, then a submarine depot ship moored off Rothesay, Isle of Bute. We seamen were in a big messdeck forward, with a long wooden table and benches for each mess of about 20 men. We collected food from the galley in trays and ate it on the tables (plates being kept there). The ship was infested with cockroaches and the food we got had them floating in it – it was a case of eat the food and place roach on side of plate. The older matelots used to drip rum on the deck and tables to attract the roaches – it got them a last drink before DEATH.

(C. Taylor, Ordinary Seaman, HMS *Montclare* 1953)

The Royal Navy first experimented with a 'general messing' system as far back as the early 1900s. It was conceived by one Adolph Jago, a Swiss restaurateur retained by the Admiralty to reform and update its victualling arrangements, such as they were. His was not, perhaps, the first nationality to spring to mind for expertise in the field of nautical nourishment, but no doubt his other credentials were adequate. The War Office had

HMS *Montclare*

employed Alexis Soyer in a similar capacity in the Crimea half a century
earlier, which was about as long as it took their Lordships to assimilate a
new idea. The Navy system was originally tried out in the barracks at
Devonport where, having proved beneficial to the sailor's well-being,
affording him a balanced, healthy diet and above all, proving to be cost-
effective and much more efficient than the previous arrangements, it was
retained thereafter. Henceforward, HMS *Drake*, Royal Naval Barracks
Devonport, was known to generations of 'Westoe' (West Country) sailors
as 'Jago's Mansions', in affectionate remembrance of their benefactor.

There was nothing revolutionary about general messing as a method of
feeding large bodies of men; it simply replaced the piecemeal issue,
cooking and consuming of victuals with a central galley, communal
dining halls and a properly balanced menu, together with the obvious
economies of scale. Tentatively, over decades, the system was extended to
other barracks and shore establishments and then to capital ships;
eventually, in a modified form, to cruisers and some lesser warships, but
this took many years and up to the late 1950s canteen messing was still
the rule in most destroyers and frigates. The period of transition from
one to the other could be painful:

As for the food on board, the least said about it the better. Although
the galley was working on half-shift, *Glasgow* was one of the ships

27

selected to experiment with centralized messing and the helicopter hangar was used for the purpose. We queued up to be served by the cooks, and we each had to collect a bakelite (or early plastic-type) tray on which the food was dumped. The trays, apart from being always greasy, had three or four shallow pressed-out hollows to hold the food and one's mug, but the hollows were so shallow that any gravy or custard slopped over and intermixed as well as dribbling onto the deck. The quality was very mediocre.

(J.M. Huntington-Whiteley, Writer, HMS *Glasgow* 1948)

Here the Navy was undergoing one of its periodic convulsions in its feeding arrangements: the introduction, in ships with a big enough compartment within them, of a central mess hall and cafeteria. General messing in all but the bigger ships at that date still meant that meals were dished up and eaten on the messdeck.

If I thought *Phoebe* was cramped this was worse, with all your kit in a compartment of the messdeck seating. At least previously we had a kit locker.

The food was still general mess, and still as disgusting. Our first call ashore was still always somewhere to eat, and the canteen on board did a roaring trade in tinned food and chocolate. The best of the ship's cooks were always allocated to the wardroom galley and the only way to get a reasonable meal was to be really ill and confined to a cot in the sick bay where one would, with any luck, be prescribed a wardroom diet as part of one's convalescence.

(G. Jay, Able Seaman, HMS *Corunna* 1950)

Remembering that rationing was still in force and that service personnel were entitled to more than civilians, I have to say that we should not have complained but, as servicemen always have and no doubt always will, we did. Our meals of those days would either see today's Navy with a mass mutiny on its hands, or with no volunteers! Porridge was anything between a kind of 'Oliver's gruel' which was poured like barley-water out of the ladle – or whacked down on the plate by the server from shoulder height in order to eject the solid ball of plaster of Paris-type stodge, with no vestige of 'cow-juice'. Cornflakes were indeed just that, though dry. They tasted rather like slivers of strawboard and when mixed, sparsely floating about in an almost colourless, grey-white fluid they looked, and tasted, like autumn leaves floating in gutter-rainwater! We bet odds that the same hand that mixed the water to our rum was also that which had adulterated whatever kind of milk it had originally been – possibly water buffalo?

One thing I will always give the Andrew – when they baked their own bread it was super stuff; in later years I was lucky enough to serve on several of the 'bigger jobs' which had their own bakeries. There were no ready-sliced loaves at that time and to make the bread go further each loaf was put through a bacon-slicing gadget, with the resulting slices on large plates at invervals along each wooden mess table where a large number sat, bum to bum and shoulders overlapping, down each side. Someone would have calculated that there would be enough for two slices per man, but human nature being what it is there were always the greedy, the practical jokers, or simply the first to get to the trough – and 'devil take the hindmost'.

(M. Bree, Writer, HMS *Woolwich* 1949)

In the opinion of one senior officer, 'Ashore and in large ships general messing was, with reservation, reasonably popular, its quality dependent on the ability of the paymaster commander and the ships' cooks to please everybody all the time; canteen (standard ration) messing was the norm in smaller ships. Arrangements at sea for sleeping, eating and washing had hardly changed since 1919; even in new construction ships fitted with recreation spaces habitability was not impressive.'[2]

The latter assertion, at least, is indisputable, and the assessment of general messing is fair, with its somewhat lukewarm (like the food when it reached the messdeck) 'with reservation' and 'reasonably popular'; though those reservations were put more colourfully by disgruntled recipients, as we have seen. Still, general messing was, beyond doubt, an improvement on canteen messing; rather more twentieth century with three meals a day planned and prepared by those whose job it was, rather than by a seaman torpedoman or aircraft mechanic. This officer is on firmer ground with a further development, that of 'centralized messing':

After successful trials in the fleet carrier *Implacable* in 1944 centralized messing was introduced in all new aircraft-carriers, the latest cruisers and some battleships. This entailed building dining-halls and serveries next to galleys so that the whole ship's company could be fed with pre-plated meals during a continuous sitting. For the first time in naval history, food, messtraps and washing-up facilities were removed from messdecks, fulfilling a long-standing request of older ratings. It was of particular advantage to aircrew requiring round-the-clock sustenance but due to lack of space it could not be applied to small ships. Nevertheless, it was a promising step forward in modernizing the archaic methods of feeding sailors.

Amen to that. This account reveals that centralized messing was experimented with at an early date – during the war, in fact – but it was to be many years before the system was established in any but the handful of new major warships laid down towards the end of, and immediately after, the war. There were very few of the older ships in service which were capable of adaptation for the reasons already stated; any space to spare below decks being needed for new weaponry and its associated systems. As we have seen, there was little to spare as it was, least of all to increase Jack's share of it. This had been less perhaps the admirals' fault than that of their in-house experts, the élite corps of naval constructors, warship designers whose design philosophy was rooted in the Dreadnought era.

No chapter on Jack's daily sustenance can be complete without reference to the rum issue, 'the matelot's built-in stablizer' as it has been called.[3] Since that momentous day in the history of the Royal Navy, Friday, 31 July 1970 – dubbed 'Black Tot Day' by the *Daily Express* of the time – the rum ration has become but a fragrant memory and there can be few, if any, of those matelots left in the service to mourn its passing.

The earliest recorded issue of rum to a man-of-war's crew was in Jamaica (where else?) in 1655. This issue was not sanctioned by authority, but was an expedient resorted to by the local commander whose ships had only foul water and sour beer remaining in their casks to drink. It was largely because rum kept better – indeed, it improved with keeping – that its use spread gradually throughout the fleet to replace the old ration beverages of beer, or wine, or brandy. The ration had been at one time as much as a pint a day – of neat, high-proof rum! The problems caused by such a prodigious daily issue of ardent spirit hardly need enumerating here, and the ration was progressively reduced over three centuries; ultimately to a half-gill (about equivalent to two public-house doubles), even this diluted, for junior rates, by the addition of two parts water (grog).

'Up Spirits!' signalled the collection by the appointed ones of each mess from a central distribution point of the daily rum ration, then as traditional a part of the day as the 'Sunset' ceremony that ended it or the reveille that began it. Whenever the bosun's call made a pipe it was followed by a verbal clarification; on ship or shore everywhere the announcement 'Up Spirits!' would always bring forth a chorus of, 'Stand fast the Holy Ghost!' one of those traditional things, the origin of which was lost back in time, but which every new sailor carried on. Until we became 'entitled to draw', we only knew of the long tradition of this 'grateful gift' to the Navy from the people of the West Indies in return for 'ridding their seas of the scourge of piracy'.[4]

The daily tot, especially at sea on long voyages, made a very welcome highlight in what could be monotonous days – and it also had many sideline benefits. Those 'of age' who did not, for religious, moral, medical or any other reason wish to partake of 'the nectar of Neptune' need not do so, and for their temperance were paid 3*d* (1½p) per diem. A special 'Request' had to be made and passed through the due processes to make or cancel such an option and every change was noted on the rating's service certificate and pay documents.

At each daily issue the authorized quantity was taken from store by a senior stores' branch rating under the supervision of the officer of the day and a member of the regulating branch (ship's police) to be issued either neat or mixed with two parts water (grog) at the time of issue. Only petty officers and above drew neat rum; junior rates had grog unless they were ashore on duty at the time of issue, when on their return they would report to the regulating office. The officer of the day would have to leave whatever he was doing (and made his displeasure plain) and attend to watch the rating down his tot of neat rum. This was to prevent illegal hoarding (watered rum would not keep).

The tot was also a useful form of currency – a bribe for those seeking a favour and payment for a service rendered, or a form of gambling token. It was also a customary birthday present to give one's 'oppo' or messmate a sip, or more, of one's 'bubbly' on the appropriate day. Now, sadly gone, like much else in the shrinking, all-but-vanished, 'New Navy'.

M. Bree, Leading Writer, HMS *Woolwich* 1949)

A tot's greatest value though – at least, in this writer's opinion – was as a palate-blunter before one's dinner.

It has to be allowed that our major ally seemed to get along well enough without a daily dose of Nelson's blood; or what in their case would presumably have been, had they had such a thing, 'John Paul Jones's blood'. But they did not lack other comforts:

Some weeks after Exercise Mariner I was part of a liaison team to exchange ships. I was allocated to the USS *Iowa*. To us it was like living in the Ritz: sleeping in bunks with sheets, eating in a restaurant-like mess with as much chicken and steak as you could eat (we only had chicken at Christmas in those days). Patrolmen walking the ship with loaded pistols – who were they going to shoot? Before she fired her 16 in guns a bell went ding-ding and then came the biggest bang I'd ever heard. It cleared the wax out of our ears alright.

(G. Whybrow, Leading Telegraphist, HMS *Barossa* 1953)

We picked up two Yank chiefs from a carrier as we were going back to Subic Bay for mail. The first breakfast was 'Mad Woman's * * * *'.[5] As usual most people had toast instead, but these two scoffed all they could get and then some from the POs' mess. Asked why they enjoyed it so much they said, 'In our goddamn navy all you get is chicken four times a day!' As we had not, at that stage, seen chicken at all on our menus, we of course considered it a luxury.

(R. Jamieson, CPO Coxswain, RAN 1964)

It just goes to show: 'one man's meat . . .'.

CHAPTER THREE

Both Watches Fall In, Clean Ship!

The work of a ship's company on a warship in harbour could be categorized as essential and non-essential, or make-work. In the first category the engine-room and electrical-branch ratings had their maintenance routines; the seamen, daily cleaning duties about their parts of ship and messdecks, which consisted both of scrubbing – decks, paintwork, woodwork – and painting. Except for boats' crews and a small boatswain's party which performed minor repairs and maintenance of ship's gear, few postwar ratings were involved with 'seamanship' as their predecessors knew it. Major repairs and replacement of standing and running rigging, anchors and cables and bottom-cleaning were now carried out by dockyard staff.[1]

In the second category fell, among other things, the loathed task of polishing the large number of brass fittings – known as 'brightwork' – to be found aboard all warships. Brass 'tallies', or nameplates, studded bulkheads above and below decks: the bridge and chartroom had more than their share, together with binnacle cover, ship's bell and alarm gongs. Most guns were fitted with brass tampions and muzzle-bands; these served no purpose and were purely for display. Brightwork was cleaned with a tin of metal-polish known as 'Bluebell', the famous brand name with which Victorian skivvies were familiar, and handfuls of cotton waste, bales of which were kept in the boatswain's store.

Such time-consuming titivation was another result of the regular naval officers' determination to return to the pre-war status quo of scrubbed decks, gleaming brasswork and snow-white canvas. At the outbreak of war, other priorities intruding, the Admiralty issued an order for all brasswork to be hidden under the standard dark grey dockyard paint known as 'crab fat'. Thus it remained throughout the hostilities, without discernible effect on a crew's morale or efficiency. Following VJ Day, ships re-stored with cotton waste and Bluebell, and Jack turned to again, sucking his teeth. First lieutenants of ships slow to do so were blasted by choleric inspecting Admirals for neglect of duty.

Slowly, painfully slowly, attitudes began to change. Speaking of the period 1945 to 1955, concerning shipboard work routine, a senior naval officer puts the new thinking, not too lucidly, into words: '. . . For example, why should you scrub a piece of wood in order to make it shine every morning, when it contributed little or nothing to the improvement of the ship? Either the wood could be something which didn't need scrubbing all the time or the routine of doing it could be so worked into your daily life that it wasn't simply one of those horrible chores you had to do every day. Similarly, there were certain things which, nice as they would be to do, the ship would not suffer noticeably if you didn't do them. In other words, unnecessary work.'[2] The writing was on the wall for brightwork.

Such englightenment was no doubt fostered by a shortage of manpower, given the Navy's difficulties in recruitment and retention. One place where such shortage was not a problem, and where 'make-work' was the daily norm because of a large transient population of ratings between sea drafts or awaiting training courses, was Royal Naval barracks, or 'Depot'. There was an RNB at each of the home ports of Devonport, Portsmouth and Chatham.

> I was detailed off for the Depot Working Party, like most new joiners, and given a canvas armband with 'DWP' in big black letters on it. This was so that the Barrack Guard, who were known as the Gestapo and always on the lookout for skivers, could keep tabs on you. Every morning at 'Hands Fall In' you were mustered in the Drill shed and detailed into parties for coal-humping, gash-bin emptying and so on. When you were told off for a job they took your station card off you so that you couldn't skive off. This was known as the Slave Market.
>
> (J. Owen, Ordinary Seaman, HMS *Drake*, RNB Devonport 1949)

As a young able seaman, I had a similar experience of *Drake's* slave market. Being detailed with several others for work in the depot salvage hut, we were doubled away by a leading hand. The salvage hut proved to be a ramshackle wooden building in a remote corner of the barracks; too remote for the Commodore's weekly rounds to judge by the litter and general scruffiness which surrounded it. It was here that the depot's non-perishable waste was brought to be sorted, bagged and baled for collection weekly by a civilian contractor. This was, of course, long before right-minded people worried about rain forests and the planet's finite resources – we had nuclear annihilation to worry about then. It was still called 'salvage' at that time, as it had been during the war, and was collected for the same reason – scarcity of raw materials, which cost dollars.

My fellow-conscripts were set to work emptying large sacks of waste-paper into a hopper and operating a creaking wooden baling machine which resembled a Roman siege engine and strenuously worked by what looked like capstan bars. I was led to a dark, dusty corner and motioned to sit on a low wooden stool – it was, in fact, an old NAAFI chair with the back struts knocked out and the legs sawn down – with a cushion of sacking stuffed with cotton waste. Placed before it was a paving slab mounted on loose bricks, on which lay a light hammer. On the floor beside this makeshift workbench was a plywood box; on the other side, a foot-high pile of used toothpaste tubes. My job was to take a tube from the pile, removing and discarding the plastic cap if this had not already been done by the erstwhile consumer, hammer the tube flat on the stone – which action never failed to produce a last little squirt of toothpaste, however well-squeezed the tube – and drop it in the box (toothpaste tubes of that date, one should explain, were of soft metal rather than plastic, with a high lead content; something else that did not seem to worry anyone). The pile was replenished from time to time by those whose job it was to dredge for toothpaste tubes. Rotten teeth with bloody roots frequently turned up in the dental surgery refuse.

I carried on this Third World activity for some three weeks before effecting my escape by volunteering for a training course. The best that could be said for it was that I ended my working day smelling of nothing worse than peppermint, which was more than could be said for some of my fellow toilers. On completion of the course I was reassigned to the daily slave market and, having in my absence been replaced by another toothpaste-tube salvor, invariably found myself among the 'gash hands' remaining after the morning details, like the rabbits whom nobody picks for a football game at school. We were usually put to sweeping roads, which is what my physics master, Mr Poole, always said I would end up doing.

At least work aboard ship was for some, more varied, with the many branches and specialisms available. As previously mentioned, much of this work was routine maintenance of machinery and equipment, and was overseen by the appropriate heads of department: engineering, electrical, radio and so on. Even some of the 'dab-toe' seamen would be members of the gunner's or torpedo parties, employed on cleaning and maintenance of weapons and associated gear. Naturally, the tempo and variety of work depended on the type of ship – destroyer, minesweeper, aircraft-carrier, depot ship – and whether the vessel was active or in reserve. Flight-deck crews on carriers, for example, led very busy and eventful working lives, particularly during 'Flying Stations':

When we exercised with rocket assisted take-off gear (Ratog) the rockets were tested fitted to aircraft. The testing team was two electricians and myself; one in the cockpit and one with me in the port undercarriage wheel-well. We would carry out ohmmeter safety checks and test the firing button. On the final test I would send the electrician with me away and tell the one in the cockpit to hold the controls neutral while I placed a foot on the undercarriage structure, then with one hand gripped the wheel door structure and with the other, pressed the control-panel button. This was standard practice after one aircraft Ratog fired off and burnt the overalls off a pilot who was sitting on the tailplane waiting for the test to be completed. The aircraft travelled about 50 yards up the deck and was undamaged.

One major change we had when switching from propeller aircraft to jets was the 'Coughman' aircraft start to an external trolley accumulator, which was difficult to unplug after starting and then to get through the jet slipstream. In the early days we lost a trolley unit over the stern round-down and the Very warning pistol was set off, causing the chasing destroyer to leap into action and the tannoy at Commander (Air)'s position to blare out, 'Buck up on the flight-deck!'

One squadron – I think it was 767 – was called 'the Clockwork Mouse squadron'. The symbol on the Sea Fury was a mouse with a key in its back. They used two Sea Furies at a time and were progressively reducing the time for take-off and landing. The method used was, on landing-on, a naval airman with a tail-arm would slip the tail on and 4 or 5 handlers would arrive on each wing-leading and push back, with the tail-arm man steering the aircraft to the centre-line of the deck. This was under the control of the flight-deck officer who held up a red flag. When he was satisfied with the positioning he would raise a green flag and wave it in a rotary motion for the pilot to open the throttle and put his controls in the take-off position. When the green flag was lowered he would take off (this was all done very quickly). On one occasion the tail-arm only part-released and the tail-arm man in trying to disengage it, locked it on again. The flight-deck officer only saw it disengage and gave the go signal. The aircraft roared up the deck with tail man hanging on. The slipstream and aircraft speed made him let go, and the aircraft went off to land ashore.

(D. Harding, Leading Electrical Mechanic, HMS *Illustrious* 1950)

Any carrier's deck during take-offs and landings (particularly the latter) was the scene of intense, well-drilled activity and often, especially on a trials and training carrier, not a little metal-rending, wire-parting and general mayhem:

> I had a very lucky escape whilst I was aboard. No doubt you remember the hairy landings that those RNVR made from time to time, hitting the wire barriers or going over the side. My part of ship for a time was driver of the Captain's barge, this was a red motor boat fitted with twin P6M diesels. Its position on board was on the port boat-deck which protruded slightly out from below the flight deck. I was servicing the engines one day whilst flying was taking place and was under the engine canopy. One of the seamen crew was also on the barge, scrubbing the deck at the bows. He decided to go below for something and climbed down to the boat-deck, leaving his bucket and scrubber on the bows of the barge. He had only been gone two minutes when I heard the awful sound of a plane landing, one wheel collapsing and the metal-on-metal screech as the plane came over the side and struck the outboard side of the barge on its way to the drink. The barge was tilted over in the gripes about 30 degrees and, as I was hurled across the port engine to the window of the canopy, I could see the pilot hauling back his cockpit canopy to get out. All this was over in seconds before his plane was left astern by the speed of the ship. The pilot was happily picked up by the escorting destroyer and I believe he was uninjured.
>
> Then I heard voices shouting from the flight-deck as they realized that there was someone aboard the barge. I was not hurt, only shaken and a little bruised; I was advised to go below and rest a while. Before I could climb down from the barge, they spotted the bucket on the bows: it had not tipped over as the barge tilted and it was perched at a precarious angle with most of the water still in it. The officer in charge immediately assumed that someone had been on the bows with a bucket and took a lot of convincing that I knew the seaman had left the boat before the incident. He would only believe me after they piped for the man to report to the scene. I'll never forget the look on his face when he saw the damage and that bucket still standing there. If he had delayed his departure another two minutes he would have joined that pilot in the sea but would not have survived, the plane would have hit him on the way down.
>
> (E. Harris, Stoker Mechanic, HMS *Illustrious* 1950)

Most crashes were crashes into the barrier; they were the preferred kind as they left a bent aeroplane but, with luck, a live and merely shaken pilot. In thankfully few instances, things went horribly wrong. During my

20-month service in *Illustrious* a ship's flight pilot (i.e. not a trainee) was killed in a too-fast landing when his arrester-hook tore off, tipping the aircraft so that it ploughed forward on its nose and under the barrier, tossing it up like a bullock at a hurdle. The tautened barrier wires ground along the engine cowling and into the cockpit canopy, slicing the top of the pilot's skull as neatly as the top of a boiled egg.

While deck landings were going on, and in a training carrier that was usually all the hours of daylight, other ship's work had of course to proceed and, as we have seen from S/M Harris's account above, risk of injury or worse was not confined to the flight-deck.[3] Another fatal accident the very next day, and one which underlined the strict rule of no one being on flight-deck level during a landing (even flight-deck crewmen took refuge in the 'dips' below deck level, springing into action the moment a plane arrested) occurred when a Sea Fury missed the arrester wires, slewed to starboard and crashed into the multiple pom-pom mounting abaft the island superstructure and burst into flames. The ever-ready fire crews, like 1930s B-movie spacemen in their bulky asbestos suits, boots and helmets, lumbered in to quench the flames with gallons of spouting foam and pulled clear the shocked but intact flyer. It was only after the wreckage was removed and they were hosing away the foam that they discovered, huddled under the gun platform, the charred remains of an armourer. It was assumed that, against orders, he had carried on with his maintenance routine on the guns when 'Flying Stations' was piped and had crawled under the mounting when he saw the plane coming.

As this chapter is concerned with working conditions, mention might be made here of *Illustrious*'s heroic team of medicos, led by a junior surgeon-lieutenant who, for peacetime service, had some uniquely grisly situations to handle.

Everyone aboard an operational carrier was hard-worked; many were overworked and suffered breakdowns. At the height of the cold war there was an almost frantic urgency about *Illustrious*'s work as floating proving-ground for the Navy's air arm, soon to be tested in the skies over Korea. She spent much time at sea, 'chasing wind'. As a mere seaman, I knew little of aviation matters but it was obvious even to me that an aircraft's speed during approach and landing was crucial and, of course, a good head wind helped a lot as this made approach speed relative to wind speed down the deck, and gave 'lift'.

Having found her wind, the ship would turn her bows into it, running up speed to maximum revolutions as 'Flying Stations' was piped. Thus, with an atmospheric wind speed of say, twenty knots, combined with a head wind of thirty, there would be a fifty-knot 'brake' to assist an approaching aircraft by reducing its speed through the air from perhaps sixty knots to a mere ten. The risk of trying the reader's patience with this second-grade arithmetic is taken in order to stress the importance of a strong head wind for safe carrier landings. It need only be added that on one memorable occasion during my time aboard, a rather weary old Firefly aircraft belonging to the ship's flight actually achieved an approach speed of minus five knots and was gradually being lost astern, to Commander (Air)'s consternation and, no doubt, to the pilot's. The Captain was prevailed upon to reduce speed.

I joined *Illustrious* from *Implacable* in late August 1948, when *Illustrious* took over as trials and training carrier. I recall that it was an extremely interesting time, thanks partly to the trainee pilots and clockwork mice, but mainly to the variety of new and strange aircraft that arrived on board from time to time. These included things like the Westland Wyvern and the Short Sturgeon, as well as the Sea Vampire – which had an operational range of about a mile and a bit if I remember correctly. Somebody later tried stripping out the Vampire's landing gear to make room for extra tanks, and I believe that sea trials were conducted to see whether this high-tech contraption could be deck-landed by stalling it onto a large rubber pad. The trials pilots must have been either Japanese or drunk. I do remember seeing a light fleet carrier (*Warrior*, I think) alongside the Railway Jetty in Portsmouth with a huge Dunlopillo mattress strapped onto the aft end of the flight deck.

I also remember our taking part in two or three manifestations of Exercise 'Shop Window', which were ostensibly (and expensively) staged to give a brief taste of naval warfare to various generals, cabinet ministers, archbishops, dress designers and other representatives of the great and the good. Each exercise was a one-day event in which the ship served as a floating grandstand from which, between visits to the wardroom bar, these people could watch various demonstrations such as flight-deck operations, submarines diving, snorkelling and surfacing, destroyers dropping depth-charges and aircraft launching torpedoes close alongside. The whole thing culminated in a spectacular low-level beat up by the Sea Hornets of 801 Squadron. All very exciting.

(L. Dennis, Leading Radio Electrical Mechanic, HMS *Illustrious*)

Carrier work for naval airmen was hard and demanding, but interesting. On the other hand, messdeck living conditions in operational carriers were probably the worst in the Navy (see Harding's account on page 6).

HMS *Implacable* (sister ship of HMS *Illustrious*)

The seaman's work could sometimes be interesting too, but more often, particularly in a Home Fleet ship, it was the usual daily round of scrubbing, polishing and scraping. And painting, of course:

> I was rated ordinary seaman and given a job in my part of ship (the foretop division) which made a pleasant change from being heads sweeper, and I was anxious to make a good impression on the captain of the top – a bearded PO – who was looking for someone to paint the tripod legs of the foremast while we were alongside in Venice. Needless to say I got the job, and proceeded to clamber up the Jacob's ladder to the top of the tripod, where I rigged my bosun's chair alongside one of the legs. I then descended to collect my pot of 'pusser's grey', paintbrush, wad of cotton waste and a visit to the heads before starting on the long, solitary job of working down the first leg of the tripod.
>
> I climbed the Jacob's ladder, hauled the pot of paint up after me on the lanyard to which it was attached and placed it securely – or so I thought – on the crossbeam between two legs of the tripod, intending to leave it there until I had got myself onto the bosun's chair, with everything correctly secured and under control for my progress down the leg. I stepped onto the bosun's chair which, inexplicably, swung the wrong way. I was about 50 feet above the deck, hanging on to this pendulum by a hand and a foot. The corner of the chair just caught the full pot of paint which then plummeted deck-ward.

Unfortunately the PO with his magnificent 'set' was standing on the roof of the 268 radar office peering up at my antics, and as the pot descended it turned over, emptying its contents all over his head and beard and the upper part of his body. I was still swinging in space watching the results of my carelessness in horror and, remembering the punishments meted out to wrongdoers in *St George* and *Ganges*, I refused to come down. Eventually of course, I did, but I never saw that PO again. I was told that he went ashore that night, and on his way back to the ship fell into a canal and broke his leg. I was told that he thought I had done it on purpose as revenge for what was the worst job in that part of ship, but I couldn't help thinking that he was an ex-boys' instructor with a guilty conscience.

(G. Jay, Ordinary Seaman, HMS *Phoebe* 1947)

How many gallons of pusser's paint were applied (and spilt!) during a ship's commission! Light grey, dark grey (crab-fat), white, yellow ochre, red and green for anchor-buoys and 'tiddley'-work; varnish and enamel for the officers' quarters and bridge. As flammable stores – or inflammable, as we were once allowed to say – it was all kept, drum upon drum of it, together with serried rows of paintbrushes of every known size and shape, bales of cotton waste and a vast tank of turpentine, in the paint shop; a gloomy, odoriferous compartment furthest forrard in the ship, forward even of the boatswain's fore-peak store. Right in the bows, the paint shop was, necessarily, a tall, thin space with steeply-tapering bulkheads. It was the lair, in big ships, of an artisan painter known as 'Putty' and in cruisers and below, of an able seaman in the boatswain's party with no marked objection to a troglodyte lifestyle and a liking for, possibly even an addiction to, paint fumes. Certainly painters as a type were usually, like drunks, either comatose or belligerent.

The latter came into his blasphemous own with two periodic events in a warship's commission: Paint Ship and Admiral's Inspection. Painting a ship, from bow to stern, from truck to water-line, was done quite frequently in peacetime, when the ship's programme and her paint allowance permitted. This was particularly the case on foreign stations where warships tended to do a lot of rust-streaking sea-time, interspersed with 'flag-showing' visits to foreign ports when the ship was on display. Such painting overall, as distinct from the touching-up ministrations of the boatswain's standing 'side party' was one of those evolutions, like ammunition ship and refuelling at sea, in which all available seamen were required to take part.[4] The chief bosun's mate (the 'Buffer') was in charge, assisted by the seaman petty officer 'captains of top' in their own parts of ship.

Directly 'Both watches of the hands' was piped the boatswain's party provided bosun's chairs and 'stages': stout wooden planks some eight feet long with a short crossbeam at either end, hung over the ship's side on thick rope lanyards. Also, in preparation, a 'bowsing-in wire' would have been rigged along the forrard section of ship's side where the flare of the bows meant that a freely-hanging stage would be swinging many feet from the paintwork, out of reach of even a 'long-tom' brush. A noisy, bantering queue would form at the paint-shop hatch, each man drawing a pot of ship's-side grey paint, brush, wad of cotton waste and a length of spunyarn (a loose-laid, tarred line) to hang the pot on, amid loud and obscene remonstrations from the painter. Then each man would find his appointed place over the side, two men to a stage. Painting began, of course, at the top and worked down. A stage could be jerkily lowered by unbending the lanyard, one side at a time, and paying it out – carefully. Each pair of men would paint a 'fleet', a width of paintwork corresponding to the width of the stage plus the reach of an extended arm to either side. When the boot-topping (the black band on the waterline) was reached, the pair would be retrieved by the killick of the boatswain's party in the 'copper punt', a small, skittish dinghy built, oddly enough, of wood or plastic, and ferried to the gangway, where they would climb inboard to begin another fleet under the beady eye of the buffer, alert for messdeck skivers. ('Can I just go to the heads, chief?')

Another thing the Buffer would be beadily cognizant of was the small areas of unpainted ship's side overlooked or missed by the painters. These were known as 'holidays' and were the worst crime in the Buffer's book, though one which was all too easy to commit, with one's nose inches away from a flat, uniform grey surface. (On a stage, you couldn't stand back to admire your work.) The perpetrator would be sent over again, shinning down a lanyard and getting smeared with wet paint in the process. Work would go on all day and into the dogwatches, with an abbreviated midday break for tot and dinner, the latter usually of 'action stations' standard; corned beef and boiled potatoes perhaps, with bullet-like pusser's peas. Final touches and stowage of gear would be accomplished by men under punishment, of which there was rarely a shortage, working until dark.

Admiral's inspection took place at least once during a ship's commission. It was a minute examination of all departments by the Admiral and his staff officers and was supposed to be about efficiency, but spit and polish tended to take priority, especially on the upper deck and messdecks. Preparation for the big event began well in advance:

We were due for Flag Officer Second in Command's inspection in Hong Kong about the middle of November. I was quarterdeck division lockerman, and at the beginning of September the Jimmy (*'Jimmy the One', first lieutenant*) said our brightwork wasn't up to standard – 'a bloody disgrace' were his actual words. He wanted it taken down for buffing, all that was removable. So I had to go round and unscrew all the brass tallies and butterfly clips from the vent flaps round the after screen, dozens of them, scrape any paint off, rub them up with wire wool and bluebell until they were gleaming – it took me a week. I went to put them back, and the DO (divisional officer) told me to leave them off as they'd only get tarnished again! Then the electrical officer came down doing his nut because his electricians couldn't work out which vent was for what – talk about Harry Tate's! So I was told to put them back, but smeared in vaseline to preserve the shine.

(N. Townsley, Able Seaman, HMS *Opossum* 1954)

Much detailed forward planning for the inspection went on for weeks (and sometimes months), occupying – probably to the detriment of other matters – a disproportionate amount of the Captain's and executive officer or first lieutenant's time. There was nothing spontaneous or unpredictable about an Admiral's inspection, either as to the date of it or the form it would take. Presumably it was intended as an encouragement-cum-threat to keep a ship's company on its toes at a stage in the commission when it might have been getting stale. As a true test of efficiency, it would assuredly have been more effective had it been a snap inspection, with ships descended upon without warning. Perhaps Dartmouth-born friendships and undying loyalty to term-mates would, in practice, have precluded total secrecy.

After close scrutiny of a ship's, by now, yacht-like condition above decks and below, a succession of high-speed harbour drills would be ordered by the staff officers. These were also predictable (and therefore previously rehearsed): such things as weighing anchor by hand, rigging sheerlegs, fire and emergency drills, laying a dan buoy and nearly always, as ponderous light relief, sending the ship's cooks away in a seaboat to deliver a fried egg to the flagship. The outcome of a flag officer's inspection was of little significance for Jack – unless it was so unsatisfactory, a rare event, for a 're-scrub' to be ordered – and had more impact on an officer's annual report.

The postwar Navy was by no means all harbour routine and cleaning stations, however. When there were no 'small wars' in progress there was still plenty of work for specialized warships, principally those legacies of the recent big war, minesweeping and wreck clearance.

The work of wreck dispersal was physically exhausting, extremely demanding, bloody uncomfortable and immensely satisfying! It had purpose. I joined the ship on 28th October, 1949. She was my first ship after I completed my first proper electrical course and I was the only electrical rating carried. I just had to known my stuff.

The 'Isles' class trawlers were coal-fired with few comforts or entertainments aboard. We had four officers, one of whom was a warrant gunner; one chief mechanician, a PO Coxswain, two Stoker POs, two killicks and me. I had my own store aft on this tiny ship! Not very luxurious, but quiet and I could sling my hammock.

There are thousands of wrecks around our coasts. We had a book, a huge volume listing all known wrecks – some dating from centuries ago. The wrecks had to be cleared to 44 feet above mean low water springs. After working on them we notified the Admiralty and a survey vessel (*Scott? Shackleton? Dampier?*) came out a few weeks later (or months!) to check our work. If we had not cleared sufficiently we had to clear again. I can only remember doing one or two again.

We carried two 32-foot cutters which had been hugely strengthened, fitted with diesel engines and a quite sensitive echo-sounder with a paper trace (no one to touch it except me, other than to change the roll!). Sometimes the wrecks were marked with a buoy. They were never in the proper position; often as much as half a mile out. We had a Decca navigator (no one to touch it *including* me!) which was quite accurate but finding and pinpointing the wrecks was still time-consuming with only the echo-sounders. We had an ancient Asdic (sonar) of First World War vintage which hadn't been shipped for years. Arthur Ansell, a killick A/S rating and I got it to work, we tuned it down to near the frequency of the boat's echo-sounder. We anchored in the middle of the North Sea (miles from land!) and swept with the Asdic, and when we received a promising echo we could point the cutter in the right direction and the Asdic beam was picked up on the boat's E/S. Using this technique we could locate a wreck in twenty minutes.

Destroying the wrecks was hard work. Depth charges had to be brought up from the magazine and dragged to the quarterdeck by hand. They were lashed together in pairs (to prevent sea bed rolling) and fitted with their primers and 'bursters'. These were special detonators actuated by an explosive shock-wave. This was done by one charge being fitted with an electric detonator fired by a dynamo exploder in the cutter. This was *my* job alone!

The wrecks were marked out with 'pellets' exactly. The charges were lowered gently all the way to the bottom. They had to be within

15 feet of the electrical charge for the 'bursters' to operate properly
– or there was risk of a 'ripple', which wouldn't do much destruction.
The average number of charges in one 'blow' was between 20 and 30
lashed pairs. In shallow water (and all the North Sea is shallow) the
water column went hundreds of feet in the air! Before firing the ship
steamed at least five miles away and turned bows-on. It became a
matter of pride not to pay out much electric cable and thus be very
close to the 'blow' – 100 yards? 50? Well, no – but much more than
200 was 'chicken'. We frequently got drenched!

We caught fish – did we catch fish! Fish tend to live in wrecks –
especially conger. They can be 7 feet long, honest! Cod too can be 6 feet.
The fish were rarely actually killed; they were stunned and floated just
below the surface, After a short time they recovered, and we lost 'em.
However we always caught more than we needed and fish was very often
on the menu. One of our national servicemen was a fisherman from
Penzance and he could skin a conger in five minutes. Once we blew a
shoal of herring. The sea was absolutely white with fish! They were so
thick that fish were actually above the surface, supported by those below.
Every seagull on the east coast appeared and formed a huge round
mountain of birds. It was a sight I'll never forget – incredible!

Living in the *Steepholm* was rough. She was coal-fired and heating
in the mess was by an old Tortoise coal stove. The condensation was
tremendous and many slept with oilskins over their blankets in
hammocks. We had to 'bath in a bucket'. To get hot water you had to
go out onto the well deck and hand-pump water into the tank on the
fo'c'sle deck. Frequently someone would hear the pump being
worked, nip up, and pinch the water!

I left *Steepholm* in Liverpool on 10 March 1952 – I've looked up my
service certificate. I 'picked up the rate' (promoted) and joined
Centaur, aircraft-carrier, soon after. What a change!

(J. Crew, Electrical Mechanic, HMS *Steepholm* 1951)

Wreck clearance, like minesweeping, was indeed hard, cold and
potentially dangerous work – but with what zest, and proper pride in
doing a worthwhile job, is it described! This was a rating entered as a boy
seaman who was not fulfilled by endless deck-scrubbing and brass-
polishing and who was persistent enough, and lucky enough, to be
enabled to follow his technical bent. As an electrician he was a key
member of *Steepholm*'s crew, experienced real responsibility for the first
time in his naval career, and relished it.

A separate electrical branch was of recent foundation (in fact, 1948): a
warship's electrics, until they became more sophisticated, were the

responsibility of the torpedo branch. As the young branch expanded it was possible for a few seaman ratings, given some education and aptitude, to transfer.

> my endeavours to transfer for training as a Radar Mechanic were approved and I was seconded to the ship's electrical branch to work with the radar/radio maintenance staff for the remainder of the commission, when on arrival back in the UK I was promised a draft to HMS *Collingwood* to join a course for Radar Mechanic training.
>
> Unfortunately, before we arrived back at Chatham the rate of Radar Mechanic became obsolete and the electrical branch proper had been formed with Radar Artificers and Radar Electrician's Mates taking their place. All training places were over-subscribed at *Collingwood* so I elected to train as an Electrician's Mate at the electrical school in Chatham barracks, which was my only chance of electrical training. So began the second phase of my 24 years of naval service.
>
> (G. Jay, Able Seaman, HMS *Phoebe* 1949)

A couple of years later Jay, now an electrician's mate, was drafted to HMS *Corunna*, a battle-class destroyer in the home fleet. He makes an observation concerning a little-known element in naval affairs of those years: little-known because the Admiralty was fairly successful in keeping it from the public domain:

> The spell on *Corunna* was pleasant enough despite the conditions below decks and occasional acts of sabotage. I was always surprised by the number of communist sympathizers on the lower deck in those days (early 1950s) but they were gradually winkled out.

As a member of the electrical branch he would certainly be more aware of such incidents than his shipmates. At the height of the cold war, communist sympathizers were legion among the ranks of the trade, both naval and civilian, following the then leaders of the Electrical Trades Union, many of whom were notoriously pro-Soviet, if not active communists. Naval ratings were forbidden membership of trade unions, but some junior ratings in the branch were covert members. Such subversive individuals were probably known to naval intelligence and the security services, and kept a beady eye on. I encountered evidence of this when, as a boy seaman officer's servant in a home fleet destroyer in the late 1940s, I saw a telegram prominently headed SECRET carelessly left by the master on the desk in his cabin. It named a known communist and suspected agitator in our ship's company. He was soon put ashore with his kit bag and hammock, en route to RNB, and we saw him no more.

Electrical Branch officers tended to be, understandably, slightly paranoid concerning sabotage. A few years later when I was captain of the forecastle in a frigate on the Far East station and had set the hands to chipping paintwork on the forrard screen during preparation for Admiral's inspection, our lieutenant commander (L) accosted me in a state of high agitation. He was barely coherent and obviously holding me responsible for something; and I followed him with some trepidation to the area of bulkhead which was being worked where, with a shaking finger, he indicated some lead-insulated wiring which had been nicked by chipping hammers. He seemed convinced that this was deliberate sabotage and blasted me for allowing it to happen while my sailors, as loyal to the Crown as they were ham-fisted, looked on bemusedly with furrowed brows and open mouths.

Considering what Jack had to put up with, not least from a significant minority of his officers, it is perhaps surprising that so few junior ratings were infected by communism in those politically turbulent years. But he was never a political animal and there was no real danger of a 'P' for politics being added to the other three.

CHAPTER FOUR

Fall Out The Officers!

It would be difficult for any man (or, as it must now be added, woman) serving in today's Royal Navy, to comprehend the yawning social gulf which divided wardroom from lower deck forty years ago. To a newly-joined junior rating, a naval officer really was almost a god-like figure; an imperious and condescending being whose dress and accent, no less than the comparative opulence and spaciousness of his quarters, set him far apart from the common sailor. The rating, as his greenness wore off, was sometimes shocked to glimpse feet of clay. The social gulf was, as it had always been, wider in big ships than in small, but even in the latter, the peacetime barrier soon clanged down and it was as if the recent war had never been.

The social standing of a naval officer in British society between the wars was considerable, with the wardroom the jealously-guarded preserve of the upper and upper-middle classes. Earlier in the century unsuccessful efforts had been made by the warrant officers to secure an avenue to commissioned rank, and as one of them wrote:[1]

> Executive Officers belonged to a certain section of the community, and what was termed 'naval families' were created, who for generations provided officers for the Fleet. This, while it was an excellent system for maintaining the highest naval traditions, had also the defect which monopolistic patronage always produces, and was in some quarters so mistaken as to lead to the fixed idea that the Navy was the close preserve of these naval families and not the property of the Sovereign and the nation.
>
> This stupid and extreme view was bluntly put to me by a lady who had shown great kindness to me: she was the mother of a sub-lieutenant with whom I had served, and discussing the matter she summed up in these terse and uncompromising words: 'I have the greatest sympathy with you personally in your desire to rise, but you have chosen the wrong service. The Navy belongs to us, and if you were to win the commissions you ask for it would be at the expense of our sons and nephews whose birthright it is.'

Such complacency was somewhat ruffled by the postwar Labour government's decree that no candidate for a commission in the Navy was to be barred 'by reason of social status, school or financial standing'. Paying lip-service to this egalitarian platitude, their Lordships announced in 1948 that henceforth up to 25 per cent of all officers would be obtained from the lower deck. Did this mean that hundreds of 'Ralph Rackstraws' with a school certificate, a passable accent and aspirations to leave behind the messdeck and 'go aft through the hawse-pipe' were to be brought forward? In the modern vernacular – get real! Note the cunning of that '*all* officers'; the target percentage was achieved, quite literally overnight, by the expedient of commissioning existing warrant officers.[2]

Additionally – whether or not as a placatory and, in the upshot, empty gesture toward their new political masters – their Lordships appeared to offer the chance of a commission to suitable boys and young seamen.

A rating selected would be summoned by his divisional officer and informed that CW (Commissioned Warrant) papers had been taken out in his name; that it was now up to him to show himself worthy of a commission in the Royal Navy, and he would henceforth be closely watched by his officers and petty officers. Reports were made annually on 'CW candidates', signed by the commanding officer, in addition to the normal ratings' conduct and efficiency reports. The CW scheme was originally a wartime measure, introduced to promote suitable Hostilities Only ratings, a significant number of whom were officer material, to sub-lieutenant RNVR.

And therein lay the rub. An RNVR commission was one thing: a temporary thing, to meet wartime needs. It was quite another to grant a regular commission to a rating, to mix (theoretically) on equal terms with Dartmouth-entered officers and gentlemen. Sadly, the postwar CW scheme proved a classic case of the comparatively many being called, and the few (if any) being chosen:

> The Navy has always had a manpower problem. It found (and still finds) it easier to recruit officers and artificers than the lower grades, so it has never offered paths of real opportunity to those lower grades. Such opportunities do exist but they are usually offered as a kind of bribe to entice re-engagement. As I write this I can hear the Dartmouth accent ringing in my ears: 'What rubbish – if a boy has the potential we'll bring it out'. But I've read an account about naval recruiting between the wars – the depression years. I'm glad that today, if a boy has potential, he has no need to enter in a lower grade at all. I have known many upper-yardman candidates.[3] All – every one – for one reason or another were rejected. Quite a few now have university qualifications.
>
> (J. Crew, Leading Electrical Mechanic, HMS *Centaur* 1952)

This is broadly true. In eleven years' service, I encountered only two officers who had risen through CW candidature; no doubt a few others existed. (Of course, the situation is greatly changed in the present-day Royal Navy, but it is hoped that the reader will appreciate that such is the case in all the areas of lower-deck life recorded in this history.) In reality, naturally, only a tiny minority of ratings aspired to commissioned rank; to most such an ambition was risible, as they made clear by their amiable contempt for those few who did. Unfortunately, the infinitesimal success-rate reinforced this attitude. Also, as has been asserted previously in these pages, the sailor was deeply conservative – an officer was an officer, God had made him thus – and a rating elevated to the wardroom was unnatural:

> I found generally that the ex-Dartmouth officers were 'better to get along with' inasmuch as they would know their place and I would (definitely!) know mine. The officers who were promoted from the lower deck generally had the problem of 'not knowing their place', which often led to confusion. I believe too, problems often arose in the wardrooms with ex-lower deckers who again 'did not know their place' and felt generally inferior. This in turn made it more difficult for them in their relationship with ratings.
>
> (J. Leach, Boy Telegraphist, HMS *Superb* 1949)

But Jack was more concerned, in general, with how his officers treated him than how they had arrived there. 'An efficient ship is a happy ship' was the naval officer's favourite platitude, hackneyed but true. Certainly an unhappy ship was unlikely to be an efficient one, and for a ship to be efficient, with a contented and motivated ship's company, depended more upon the calibre of her officers than on any other factor.

The happiest ship I served in happened to be my first – a Home Fleet destroyer. In a small ship such as she was, the most important member of the wardroom so far as the sailors were concerned, the one with the most impact on their daily lives and notwithstanding the captain, was 'Jimmy', the first lieutenant and executive officer. *St James* was fortunate in her first lieutenant. He was a much-decorated ex-submariner, a lieutenant-commander who had somehow – astonishingly to his devoted sailors – failed to clear the promotion hurdle to commander. This did not seem to trouble him, though such failure (about which more below) effectively spelt the end of a naval officer's career. This insouciant war hero, a pocket Hercules as dapper and small in stature as he was lion-hearted, had no time for the customary 'them and us' of wardroom and messdeck (perhaps it was his unconventional approach to man-management which outweighed the DSO and three DSCs in the promotion stakes). To provide an instance: a not infrequent pipe to be heard aboard a warship was 'Clear lower deck, hands to muster on the quarterdeck', for an announcement or briefing from the captain, or for a punishment warrant to be read. The entire ship's company apart from essential watchkeepers would lay aft; petty officers separate from junior rates and the officers grouped about the captain. With all hands asembled, the coxswain saluted the first lieutenant and reported 'Correct'; the latter did likewise to the Captain. Hands stood at ease to hear the briefing etc., on completion of which they came to attention again as the captain departed in a flurry of salutes. The ritual then was for the first lieutenant to dismiss the ship's company by ordering 'Carry on the officers!' (officers saluted him and quit the scene); 'Carry on chief and petty officers!' (chiefs and POs did likewise) and, finally, 'Carry on junior rates!' But our Jimmy would pause, as the last petty officer-like back disappeared behind the after screen, and a grin would crease his handsome features as he surveyed his sailors, grinning back at him. Curling his lip in simulated commissioned disdain, he would order: 'Carry on the gash!' A loud ironic cheer erupted as the hands broke ranks and dispersed.

This officer was respected more, not less, on the lower deck for his humanity and fellow-feeling, though it took a special kind of leadership quality not granted to every naval officer. The hands would do anything for him, and *St James* was a very efficient ship indeed, favourite of the Commander-in-Chief so we got all the best jobs. Our captain was wise enough to let Jimmy have his head in handling the sailors.

Here, on the other hand, is an unhappy ship, nearing the end of its foreign commission:

Returning home to pay off from the Far East, we were diverted at short notice to the Gulf, stopping and searching Arab dhows, finally to Aqaba. While we were here, somehow the captain 'lost' his one and only uniform cap – think it was flung over the side but nobody ever found out. However, lower deck was cleared. The captain demanded that anyone who knew anything to step forward, firmly promising 90 days' DQs (*Detention Quarters*). No movement. Made to stand to attention for quite a while, very hot. Next, a crash locker-search, everyone to turn out lockers and cases in front of divisional officer and PO. Ship searched, no hat. Beer issue stopped. Everyone in turn to DO's cabin to sign a hastily-printed slip declaring no knowledge of whereabouts of said hat or any perpetration of any action concerning said hat (shades of Captain Queeg of *Caine Mutiny*).

The following morning at the 'Hands to muster' pipe nobody moved, remaining smoking, drinking tea, rabbiting. To my knowledge it was not organized. My job was Gunner's yeoman so I didn't have to fall in. 'Hands fall in' was piped again. No movement. The Buffer appeared on the messdeck.

'Come on, you heard the pipe – get fell in!' he bellowed. Totally ignored.

'What's going on?' he demanded. Out of a cloud of Woodbine smoke a voice was heard:

'Nothing! – till *we* get our beer back and *they* get some common sense!'

Buffer departed aft. Fifteen minutes later, over the tannoy came the announcement that beer issue would be restored and hands would be required to turn to in 10 minutes. This time they did.

(R. Grevett, Leading Seaman, HMS *Modeste* 1958)

Comment seems superfluous. The Royal Navy was a demanding service for its officers and it is perhaps not surprising that the strain sometimes showed. Competition for promotion, especially in the executive, or seaman, branch was fierce. Given that his reports were satisfactory and that he passed all his examinations in due time, the Dartmouth-trained midshipman progressed automatically to sub-lieutenant and then lieutenant, with opportunity to earn enhanced seniority in those ranks by scoring high marks in exams or other displays of merit. Soon after reaching lieutenant, the young officer would have a crucial choice to make – which specialism to enter. The choices open to him were gunnery, torpedoes, signals, navigation or navigation/direction (for aircraft direction duty in carriers) or the very specialist Hydrographic Branch, responsible for surveying in the compilation of Admiralty charts. Or he could choose not to specialize, and become what was known as a 'salt horse', though these were rare indeed in the postwar Navy. The choice was more crucial than it need have been because of the extraordinary predominance, lasting for decades, of the gunnery specialism among captains and flag officers. It dated from the Dreadnought era when capital ships were floating gun platforms and a ship was judged by its performance in endless practice shoots. This emphasis on gunnery was justified in 1914–18, between the wars and to a lesser extent in 1939–45 when some big-ship surface actions were still being fought. But the Battle of the Atlantic and the Battle of Midway had demonstrated, even to the Royal Navy, the importance of anti-submarine warfare and naval aviation in any future conflict.

Despite this, for years after the Second World War, gunnery was still first choice for the ambitious young officer, who had no reason so far to doubt that it remained the royal road to promotion and a gilded peak to his cap. As a consequence, competition for selection for the gunnery Long Course at Whale Island, HMS *Excellent*, the Navy's famed mecca of the art and science of gunnery – as Jack would have it, 'gas and gaiters' – was very keen indeed and many were disappointed. At least one senior officer held the view that the cult of specialism, particularly the gunnery specialism (he was a signals officer) was inappropriate in a modern fleet, and on becoming a Board member was able to do something about it, shifting the emphasis to all-roundism. As he writes: 'Since the subject of gunnery officers seems to have encroached into this narrative, I would remark only that this admirable fraternity enjoyed, and indeed often earned, a predomiance in the higher ranks of the Navy over many years. This tends to become self-perpetuating, since able and ambitious young officers would naturally elect for gunnery when they could. The changes . . . I was fostering make this a matter of historical interest only.'[4] How cutting, that 'often'!

After eight years as lieutenant – sometimes less where extra seniority was awarded – the last automatic promotion, to lieutenant-commander, was reached. Soon after came the most critical stage in a naval officer's career, when after three years as lieutenant-commander he entered the promotion zone for commander; the golden gateway to high command. Even for the officer who retired as Admiral of the Fleet, this promotion was more crucial than any subsequent ones. For that majority of lieutenant-commanders who were passed-over, early retirement and a stab at a new career was the best option, for there were few sadder sights to the eyes of a sensitive rating than an ageing two-and-a-half ringer serving out his time as command anti-gas officer or port division welfare coordinator.

In a work concerned with the lower-deck experience, there is a point to the foregoing brief perambulation through the officer's career structure, and it is this: selections for promotion were made by an Admiralty board twice a year, at the end of June and the end of December. A lieutenant-commander remained in the promotion zone for six years; he thus had twelve chances. Most officers would entertain no real hopes for the first couple of years in the zone, and would scrutinize the half-yearly lists out of curiosity rather than expectation. Tension began to increase thereafter, and the state of mind of an officer as his final chances came and went may be imagined, as he saw his Dartmouth term-mates promoted while he languished. This system might appear tantamount to sadism as far as the officer was concerned, but it could be pretty unpleasant for sailors, too.

There can be few ex-regular ratings who have not had the misfortune to share a ship or shore establishment with one of these last-chancers. No doubt they could be beastly to their wardroom colleagues also, but certainly some – not all – took it out on Jack. While serving in an aircraft carrier in the early 1950s, I had one as a first lieutenant; in my view a particularly nasty example who, at the best of times, looked upon ratings as an unpleasant necessity and did not strive to dissemble his feelings. He was generally detested, loathed and feared by the seamen who bore the brunt of his frequent icy rages. If he was aware of it he would have been indifferent, or more likely, taken it as further proof of his efficiency, and why couldn't the blind fools see it? As a radar plot rating, I was fortunate not to come under his direct supervision but, in harbour, I was duty coxswain of one of the ship's boats. On one occasion the ship anchored, after the day's flying, off Bangor in Northern Ireland. Late in the evening I was ordered inshore to bring off a party of our officers, among whom was the first lieutenant. I embarked them at the jetty and headed out to the ship. Midway between ship and shore, some half-mile offshore because of her shallower draught, *Ulster*, our attendant destroyer, lay at anchor. It happened that her captain, a lieutenant-commander in command, was among the party. As I approached *Ulster*'s gangway her quartermaster, in accordance with regulation and custom hailed me: 'Boat ahoy!'. I called in reply, '*Ulster*!' This indicated to him that his captain was aboard my boat and, again in accordance with naval custom, the side-party was summoned to pipe him aboard as was his due. (As a matter of interest, had I one of *Ulster*'s officers aboard other than the captain, my response to the hail would have been 'Aye, aye', and if no one commissioned was embarked, 'No, no'. Another small nugget of naval arcana.)

I then continued on to my ship, stood at the salute in the stern-sheets while the officers disembarked at the after gangway ladder and then, being ordered by the officer of the watch to secure, tied up my boat to the lower boom and, together with my crew, clambered inboard. A side-boy awaited me on deck, to tell me I was to report to the officer of the watch (OOW). I went aft to find a white and shaken OOW, an elderly signal boatswain who, wide-eyed, asked me what I had done to upset Jimmy. 'He's got a right weed on. He wants to see you right away outside his cabin', he breathed, with a 'rather you than me' look. I made my way down to the cabin flat, anxiously speculating on what I had done to antagonize the first lieutenant; not a difficult thing to do at any time. My boat-handling? An uncoiled bow-line? An unshaven stoker? I wasn't even warm.

At his cabin doorway I nervously cleared my throat and croaked, 'First Lieutenant, sir?' The curtain was whisked back and this officer, clad in his dressing-gown and nearly incoherent with rage, demanded to know how long I had been a coxswain, and declared that I was unfit to be in charge of a ship's boat as I seemed to be unaware that nothing was done in or by a boat without the permission of the senior officer embarked. All this abuse and more was hurled at my uncomprehending head. It was late into the night, it had been a long day and I had no idea what he was driving at. Before casting off from Bangor jetty I had certainly put my head under the canopy, caught his eye and none other, saluted and asked, 'Carry on, sir, please?' and been answered with a curt nod. Light dawned when he demanded:

'You knew I was the senior officer in that boat?'

'Yes, sir'.

'That includes the captain of *Ulster*, and you had absolutely no right to go to *Ulster* first without my permission to do so!'

So that was it. I was the unwitting victim of promotion-zone paranoia. Passing yards from the gangway of his rival's ship – a rival who was junior to him yet had his own command and was surely a front-runner in the promotion stakes – I had taken it upon myself to go alongside without one of those condescending little nods of his. Now a warship's boat carried many items of equipment for which the coxswain was responsible: boat's compass, flares, grappling iron, fire extinguisher – but I never had charge of one which carried a copy of the current Navy List. Having unloaded the burden of his resentment, frustration and bile onto my unworthy head, my superior brusquely dismissed me and I went for'ard to the frowsty refuge of the messdeck and my hammock, feeling I now understood the significance of the faint smile on the lips of *Ulster*'s captain as he courteously tipped his shore-going soft hat in returning my salute as he disembarked. I am happy to report that this officer was promoted in the next list and our insufferable first lieutenant not until six months after that, so who was the senior now, eh?

My own divisional officer in that ship was, by contrast, a gentleman in every sense, being a scion of an old landed family; and a vague, kindly, middle-aged man who had long since passed through and beyond the promotion zone. This probably mattered less to him, with his lineage, than to more insecure, middle-class officers with something to prove. 'Daddy' Verney spent much time during the many quiet periods in the operations room engrossed in his own preoccupation, closely perusing a huge leather-bound volume as big as a family Bible, and occasionally making notes. I stole a look at it once when he was called away; it was the complete genealogical history of the Verneys and related families, liberally illustrated with coloured armorial bearings, hatchments and escutcheons. Some of the young lieutenants, too, would unbend a little toward young leading seamen in whom they recognized aspirations not unlike their own, but of course on a different level. But this promotion-zone syndrome was all too common. Here is another example:

Charles Gratton: I first came across him when I was on the *Cook*. This was in 1951, she was a new ship then. These survey ships all have wooden decks, which need scrubbing of course. Well, we had a nice little routine of scrubbing after breakfast. But the first thing Charlie said when he joined as first lieutenant – he was lieutenant-commander even then – was, 'You will scrub decks from six till seven', regardless of the weather and regardless of the time of year. So there we were, scrubbing decks in Devonport dockyard at six o'clock on a winter's morning, which didn't go down too well. So we knew then what sort of character we were dealing with.

That next season I got my draft chit out to HMS *Dampier* in the Far East. Shortly after I got out there, who should come out but Charles C. Gratton, as lieutenant-commander in command. Our routine there was: the ship used to refit in Hong Kong from November, and back down in Singapore about April. From April to August off Borneo, then back to Singapore for a short refit or Admiral's inspection. Then we'd do east coast of Malaya. Gratton was in command when we first went down to Borneo. A survey ship can't carry four months' supply of fresh meat and vegetables, and there's no chance of re-storing. All we could get from ashore was potatoes and spinach, so we weren't very happy with the food. Survey ships worked damned hard, if I say so myself – you are out in the boats from early morning till evening and then the next day's work to prepare for. There wasn't much ashore, just the ex-pats club which didn't cater for an influx of matelots and the members did not trouble to make us welcome. We did organize the occasional banyan party.[5]

We were a discontented ship's company – sparse, monotonous food, little shore leave and very hard work. Before returning to Singapore that first season, we had a job to do at a place called Bakapit. The job was such that we had to do 10-second sounding. This involves taking a sextant-angle fix every ten seconds. Hard graft – try doing that for hours at a stretch; it is very, very tiring. Not only that – you have to take extra bods out of the ship. So in one survey boat you've got the coxswain, surveying officer, two surveying recorders, an extra seaman reading the echo-sounder, another one writing down and a bowman and stoker. So in one survey boat you've got eight men and with four boats away at once there's not many

1 *Space allocated to men (aircraft-carrier's messdeck ready for Captain's rounds) . . .*

2 *. . . and machines (aircraft hangar in the same ship).*

3 'Cook of the mess' rolling pastry for a 'clacker'.

4 Writers' mess, HMS Duke of York, 1949.

5 *Happy Christmas! Sailors full of seasonal cheer smile for the camera aboard HMS* Mermaid, *Malta, Christmas 1953.*

6 *Modern training hulk. HMS* Imperieuse *(battleships* Valiant *and* Renown*) moored off Torpoint (see Chapter 8).*

7 *Old training hulk. HMS* Foudroyant *in Porchester creek, with laid-up escort vessels in background.*

8 Ships of the fleet assemble for the Coronation Review at Spithead, June 1953.

9 HMS Phoebe *light cruiser, taking part in close-formation exercises in the Mediterranean, 1948.*

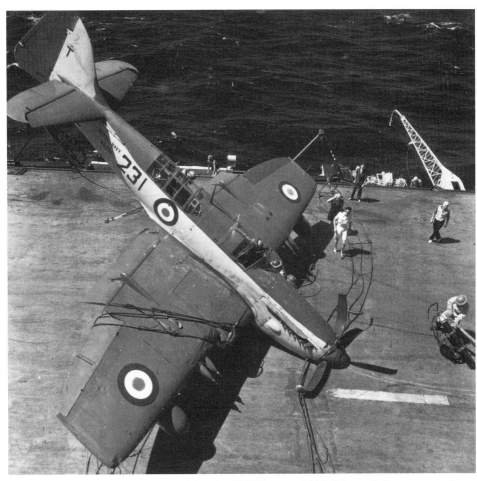

10 *A Firefly tangles with the crash barrier, HMS* Ocean, *1949. Pilot and observer escaped unhurt. Note firefighter in tin hat to right of picture, with foam apparatus.*

11 Flight of Sea Furies photographed from the bridge of HMS Liverpool *during Mediterranean Fleet exercise in 1954. The Commander-in-Chief, whose Vice-Admiral's flag may be seen at the masthead, was Lord Louis Mountbatten.*

12 *HMS Vanguard, the Navy's last battleship, red flag flying from her foremost yard-arm, fires her first, and only, broadside.*

13 HMS Kenya *in Korean waters, 1950.*

14 God, and a priest.

15 *Typical ship's company group photograph of a foreign commission, copies of which would sell briskly from the ship's canteen. HMS Mounts Bay frigate, Hong Kong, 1952.*

16 *Smart as the Guards, but not quite as tall. Guard of Honour of HMS* Chequers *awaiting HM the Queen (then Princess Elizabeth), on a visit to the ship to which Prince Philip had recently been appointed first lieutenant, in the summer of 1948.*

17 *Fleet Regatta chief and petty officers' whaler crew prepare for tow to starting line, Hong Kong, 1955.*

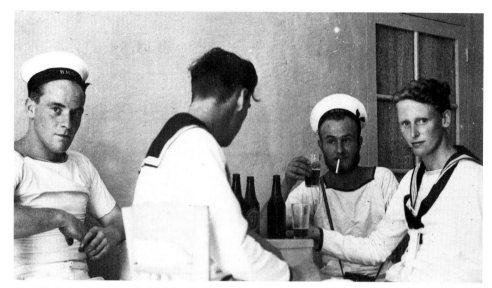

18 Jack ashore in a Malta bar. Still on their first beer, presumably.

19 A run ashore in Tripoli, 1948. Sailors soon established a rapport with children of any nationality. Or perhaps they were being offered sisters.

20 Libertymen going ashore at Harwich in the ship's tender. The two-badge killick at the centre of the group is holding in that wrapper something which is very much the size and shape of a half-pound tin of duty-free tobacco. It was said that a sympathetic ex-Navy customs boatman stationed at Harwich would display a discreet signal to warships in harbour when it was safe to land contraband.

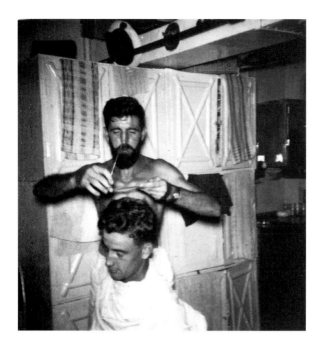

21 *Messdeck barber plies his trade.*

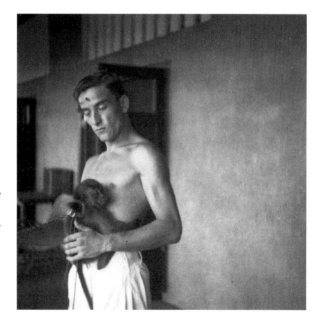

22 *One of two pets in the petty officers' mess at HMS* Terror, *naval base Singapore. The other was a crested cockatoo which ate cigarette butts and perched on the bald head of its owner.*

23 *Boy Telegraphists under instruction in a Nissen hut classroom at RN Signal School, Plymouth.*

24 *Armed boarding-party of sailors from HMS* Liverpool *cruiser ashore on Gibraltar in 1947, training for the unpleasant duty of arresting illegal immigrant ships off Palestine.*

25 *Landing-party from HMS Liverpool exercises landing at Military Bay, Malta, 1948.*

bodies left on board, especially seamen, for cleaning and maintenance.

So we'd been working hard all season and our last job before return to Singapore was Bakapit, which took us 3 weeks. Three weeks of 10-second sounding – you're absolutely whacked. Anyway we got it done and we were on our way back to Singapore – for Admiral's inspection! Then Gratton had us all aft on the quarterdeck and told us, 'You lads have done a magnificent job in completing Bakapit, but now we are going back for an Admiral's inspection and the ship is in a filthy condition. So you will work through all dogwatches until it is fit for inspection.' Well you can imagine – it was *not* a happy ship, there were mutterings and chunterings all round. We got back to Singapore, had our inspection, and we were handed a re-scrub! I think the Admiral knew there was trouble aboard because he sent some officers on his staff to talk to the ship's company. They were told straight why we were discontented and they would of course have reported back to the Admiral. And Charlie Gratton at this time, I would imagine, was sweating on his brass hat – last chance before being out of time. Not surprisingly, in view of the staff's report, he didn't get it. So things were even worse on board. He was discontented, the crew were discontented – it wasn't very happy at all.

The upshot was, the next season off Borneo they sent the *Newfoundland* down to re-store us. We'd put our complaints to the Admiral so forcefully that they made a point of sending a cruiser down just to supply the *Dampier* while we were off Borneo and couldn't carry sufficient food.

Gratton retired soon after that. I heard later that he joined a civvy surveying firm in India, where he was in charge of the native labour.

(R. Harwood, Leading Seaman Surveying Recorder, HMS *Dampier* (1953)

Survey ships were a special case, with their long hours of work for weeks on end in remote places with few shore facilities. To keep a contented ship's company in such circumstances called for a special brand of leadership from the captain and officers which was not always present. The survey fleet was almost a private navy, well out of the mainstream for promotions; the Hydrographic branch was headed by the Hydrographer of the Navy – a Rear Admiral who was the only flag officer in the branch. It was perhaps not a specialism which the most able and ambitious officers opted for, though the work was important and (for an officer) interesting; also, the officer in charge got to see his name printed on the resultant Admiralty chart. A small renown but not to be despised.

HMS *Cook*

As previously mentioned, gunnery was the favoured branch for the promotion-hungry. The Long Course gunnery officer was a quite distinct type, processed – some said brainwashed – for a whole year at Whale Island and released back to the fleet to proselytize for his branch and make Jack's life a misery.

Anyone who passed through *Ceres* at that time will also remember the Gunnery Officer – so tall and thin, with a face so angular, gaunt and bony that it resembled a skull with no more than a membrane stretched over it; a typical Whale Island gunnery school lieutenant whose long, black-leather gaiters shone blacker and brighter than our bumpered corridors; whose stiffly-grommeted cap stretched flat as a frying pan and sat exactly dead-square across his eyebrows in the fashion of the drill manual; whose thin cheeks shone at any hour of the day as though he had, just seconds before, run a highly-stropped cut-throat razor over them – a veritable paragon of parade-ground excellence. Well he would be, coming from HMS *Excellent* – he *had* to be!

No name is necessary, everybody knew him and many feared him. Few escaped his dark, beady gaze, boring from beneath the straight cap-peak like some lethal weapon. The man was regulation Navy from crown to toe caps. He knew the drill manual inside out and probably verbatim, and his only standard was perfection – or punishment. He prowled the establishment continually ('stalked' might be an apter word) like a dark Nemesis. He was everywhere at any time; no one knew where to expect him, or when not to. He was so tall and thin as to be able to lurk behind a tree trunk or telegraph pole. Known to most as 'Rip' due to sharing his surname with a well-known American comic-book hero, some had less printable soubriquets for 'Guns'. A real stick of Whale Island rock – stamped HMS *Excellent* right through!

> (M. Bree, Probationary Writer, HMS *Ceres* 1947)

The same contributor comments on the very rapid regression to the 'them and us' stand-off once the war was over:

Once the war had ended a great many things in navy life began to change – apart from the chaos already mentioned of the necessary reduction and returning thousands of men and women to 'Civvy Street'. The peacetime naval mentality soon began to reassert itself, with the martinets and bullshit merchants trying to pick up where they had left off. The 'big ships' had always been nothing more than floating barracks as far as discipline and inter-rank relations were concerned. Small ships and wartime routines etc. made for much easier, freer conditions generally, but the end of hostilities plus reorganization meant considerable change in the postwar period.

During that period, the wardroom collectively was always referred to by ratings in conversation, even where relationships were generally good, as 'the pigs' – long before this opprobrious term was first applied to guardians of the law. It was usually amiably meant, and indeed the idiosyncrasies of some of his officers afforded Jack much innocent amusement. A case in point was the Paymaster Commander of the aircraft-carrier mentioned earlier. This senior officer was in his late forties, unmarried but of a convivial disposition in a port-and-cigar kind of way. His appearance was certainly epicurean, particularly when rigged out to go ashore to one of the numerous cocktail parties, receptions and dinners he had invitations to. High living had left its mark; he was short, stout and jowly with rather protuberant eyes into one of which, when in evening dress full-fig, was screwed a gold-rimmed monocle on a black silk cord. It frequently fell out, to a soft landing on his cummerbunded paunch. His other formal-dress affectation was an item of uniform rarely seen by that date, one which would have looked dramatic and dashing on a slimmer, more virile frame, but which made the Paymaster a more risible figure than need be. It was an officer's boat-cloak, a capacious garment of finest doeskin lined with white silk, which hung from shoulders to mid-calf in soft folds, secured at the throat by a gold chain and lion's-mask clasp. It may have been mere coincidence that whenever this vision appeared at the gangway and descended ponderously to the waiting boat, the ship's SRE (internal broadcast), operated by a three-badge AB, was invariably playing Burl Ives's rendering of 'Froggie went a-courting'.

So Jack had his ways of weathering oppression and deflating pomposity, at least to his own satisfaction. Changes in attitudes were slow but inexorable, aided by a few officers of vision and influence such as one who, early in the 1950s, began at the beginning by revolutionizing the training of boys.

The best officer I ever met, one who really had the common touch yet could command respect and control better than the best of them, was the then Commander Michael J. Le Fanu. If any reader wants to know more of this human and brilliant man, read his biography *Dry Ginger*[6] which concludes with his becoming First Sea Lord and in line for even greater things but for his early death.

(J. Leach, Boy Telegraphist, HMS *Superb* 1949)

CHAPTER FIVE

Libertymen Muster at the Gangway!

All work and no play, as they say, makes Jack a dull boy. 'Jack' tended to get plenty of both in the ordinary course. Leave was normally granted to off-duty watches (three-quarters of the whole) in shore establishments and ships alongside in harbour. It began after work was secured for the day, normally at 1600 hours, and its duration depended on location, age and rank. In most UK ports all-night leave was granted to adult ratings and 'natives', expiring at 0700; boys only until 1900, young seamen until 2359, like Cinderella. In most foreign ports all-night leave was rarely granted except to chiefs and POs and, of course, officers. In shore establishments at home, and ships whose programme permitted, weekend leve was also given; either a short weekend from Saturday noon to 0700 Monday or, once a month, long weekend leave from Friday afternoon. This latter was known to Jack as a 'Friday While' (Friday while Monday) and was often utilized by an unmarried rating for a visit home to see his mother and, of course, his 'party' (girl-friend). This was assuming he could afford the rail fare; in the UK free travel warrants were provided only for the thrice-yearly 'long leave' of two weeks duration, at Easter, mid-summer and Christmas. This allocation of annual leave was, surprisingly for the Navy, more generous than that enjoyed by the two junior services.

Shore and training establishments usually closed down at leave periods, leaving behind a 'retard party' for security and maintenance, while ships in commission granted long leave in two watches. This meant that for four weeks, three times a year, an HM ship was non-operational, though it could, in theory, put to sea with half its complement ashore. In any case, leave in the Navy, as was often stressed, was a privilege and not a right, and always subject to 'the exigencies of the service'. Long leave could be, and not infrequently was, cancelled, postponed or curtailed in an emergency.

All the foregoing applied to leave allowances ashore and in home-based ships. There was no home leave for crews of warships during a two-and-a-half year foreign commission; instead, about mid-way through a commission when a ship would normally be docked for refit, local 'station leave' of ten days or so might be granted to ratings desiring it, in places where rest camp or similar facilities were present. On return to the UK, foreign-service leave equivalent to one-and-a-half days per month's absence, including time on passage, amounted to some seven weeks' leave. Once in a service lifetime, some occasion great enough to interrupt or shorten a foreign commission might take place:

> My time on *Mermaid* coincided with the Royal Fleet Coronation Review at Spithead. This proved very fortunate as we were actually listed to join the Review. So the ship came home to Portsmouth, then a full repaint job to Home Fleet grey followed by seven days leave each. Then back for the Review itself. After that, back to Gibraltar, re-paint to Med Fleet grey and finish off tour. A nice mid-commision break in my case. (R. Grevett, Ordinary Seaman, HMS *Mermaid* 1953).

To bring a ship home from a foreign station to take part in the Fleet Review, not to mention the prodigal expenditure of pusser's paint, is an indication of the much-diminished size of the Royal Navy since the previous review of 1937 and the need to put on a decent show. Granted, Gibraltar was only a few days' steaming from Portsmouth, whereas it would hardly have been practicable to bring ships home from the Far East for a two-day fixture – the Mediterranean was always contemptuously referred to as 'a f***ing weekend station' by sailors serving in more distant parts.

If another of those brief sidetracks might be permitted here: my submarine was likewise recalled from Gibraltar for the Coronation review. Shortly before we left, the captain cleared lower deck to read to us the contents of a confidential AFO (Admiralty Fleet Order) just received. It was a directive from their Lordships concerning the drill to be followed in 'cheering ship' as the monarch passed by in review at Spithead. Caps were to be removed and held at arm's length above the head and flourished in a sweeping clockwise motion three times, in phase with the cheers. The cheers were to be preceded by three 'Hips' rather than the more customary two, and followed by 'Hoor*ay*!' and *not* 'Hoor*ah*!' (The house of Windsor seemed to have an aversion to the broad 'a' sound. Years later in another capacity I was among those privileged to conduct Her Majesty round an exhibition, and was warned to address her as 'Mam' and not 'Marm' as effete English courtiers always do in Hollywood movies.) The captain made us practise it. We also practised 'manning ship' – lining the ship's side at attention as the Queen passed in the royal yacht, then about-turning to face her again as she passed down the other side. This was more difficult on a submarine than a surface ship with roomy decks and guardrails all round; we had only a narrow casing to stand on and a single jack-stay running fore and aft down the centre-line. Also, it was prudent to assume that on any great public occasion in England it would be raining – as indeed it proved – and the casing was quite slippery when wet.

The first lieutenant determined that for safety's sake the hands should wear lifelines. These he instructed me to make up from lengths of cod-line, a stores item cordage about the thickness of a washing-line. Each sailor would tie it round his waist under his jumper and hitch the loose end to the jack-stay. So far, so good. Then it was realised that the cod-line, which was a kind of off-white in colour, would show up against navy-blue clothing. I was sent ashore to purchase a stone bottle of Stephenson's blue-black ink; this was poured into a baking tray requisitioned from the galley, some thirty lifelines dipped in it and hung in the fore-ends to drip-dry. On the day they served their purpose well enough and we lost no-one over the side. But as mentioned it was raining, and the white-blancoed crown of every sailor's cap bore a perfect set of blue-black fingerprints which Cherill of the Yard would have been proud to produce in evidence.

To return to shore-leave. Foreign ports on the Mediterranean and Far East stations had their own legendary attractions for Jack ashore.

We had been out in the Med. for eight months and my wife, Mavis, came down to Devonport to meet the ship. We arranged for another wife to travel down with her. On the way down she told Mavis that her husband didn't go ashore drinking, only on excursions run by the Padre. Mavis knew I was not like that and I knew this woman's husband wasn't. Everything was going OK until I showed Mavis some photos and she passed them over. I hadn't looked at them in detail and failed to notice that one of them was taken in the Trocadero in Gib and showed a Spanish dancer surrounded by matelots drinking pints of beer. One of them was her husband.

'I'll give him going on trips with the Padre!' she said. I suppose she did give him hell! You often wonder what happened to these people. I suppose like us they're scattered all over the world.

(B. Whitworth, Leading Stoker Mechanic, HMS *Ark Royal* 1956)

At home, under the prevailing economic constraints, warships spent much of their time berthed at home ports – 'aground on 'er own milk tins', as Jack would growl. Aside from 'natives' (those crew members with a wife in lodgings at the home base for whom shore-leave was merely going home after the day's work), the bachelor sailor's ideal run ashore was 'big eats, bag-off and back on board', the Three Bs, as one might say. This is a generalization, of course. There was many a clean-living young rating with a 'party' keeping herself for him back in his home town, to whom he wrote mildly passionate letters two or three times a week and whose own pay-night run ashore would take in egg and chips and a couple of pints at the NAAFI, a visit to the cinema and a chaste bed at 'Aggie Weston's'.[1] And then there were the 'pizo' (mean, tight-fisted) ratings – every messdeck had one – who never left the ship between long leaves and whose mantra, to the tune of 'Baa, baa, Black Sheep' was: Dhobey, dhobey, dhobey, never go ashore; never have to knock at the sick bay door. . . .' (They had a point; the sisterhood which frequented the pubs and dives of Union Street, Plymouth and Queen Street in Portsmouth did much to keep the VD ward of the naval hospitals – known as 'Rose Cottage' – busy.)

Naval ratings were paid fortnightly, in cash, at the 'pay muster', when the sailor would step up to the Paymaster's table, call out his ship's book number and receive his dole, less stoppages, in notes and coins on the crown of his proffered cap – another archaic and demeaning ritual ripe for reform. Consequently, shore-going tended to be concentrated in 'pay week', with far fewer, if any, excursions during 'blank week', when Jack was usually skint. The born optimist might approach a messmate of the pizo persuasion and request a small loan 'till pay-day', (from whence sprang yet another lower deck ditty, this one to the opening bars of 'Blaze Away': 'Do us a sub (substitute for my duty on board this evening), lend us a quid (pound sterling), give us a rub (loan) of your Burberry' (uniform raincoat). It is catchier without the intrusive translations, but no more likely to be gratified.

Blank week was when shipboard activities and amusements came into their own:

> One of the most popular games allowed to all and sundry was Tombola. Nowadays this is known as Bingo. Although both names refer to the same game, their operation differed markedly. The Navy version was, in my view, much more entertaining and was always well-attended. Although winnings were rather conservative compared to today's big-money incentives, much enjoyment and hilarity was evident. On small ships, usually the Coxswain or senior chief would preside, with a well-versed and popular leading hand as the all-important 'caller'. Numbers were picked out of a well-worn leather bag, and called in a fashion peculiar to the Naval service alone. Excitement always mounted towards the end of a card, with many

only awaiting a final number. When 'House!' was called, cries of 'Fiddle!', 'Same old faces!' and 'Coxswain's bum-boy!' were rife, adding to the merriment. The fact that a rating had won a 'house' guaranteed him a good run ashore next time, and he was quite happy with that.

Ships' welfare funds benefited a lot from Tombola and other games arranged for such a purpose. Jack is nothing if not generous in any worthy cause. For instance, if a rating died from any cause while serving amongst them, they would organize an 'auction' of all his personal belongings. I have known a worn-out, virtually valueless shaving brush sold for twice its worth when brand-new; a lanyard costing 6*d* (2½p) from pusser's stores, going for £2. The widow or relative always had reason to be grateful to his messmates in their bereavement.

(F. Woods, Leading Stoker, HMS *Contest* 1951)

Tombola was the only game of chance officially condoned by the authorities (with the percentage for welfare funds mandatory) and, generally speaking, was the only one played, apart from an occasional messdeck card game for sixpences or cigarettes. The illegal Crown and Anchor was rarely seen by this date; the postwar rating tending, perhaps, to be more intelligent than earlier generations and capable of working out that he couldn't win.

There were other things to do on board in the dogwatches. The sailor has always been noted for his skill in handicrafts and his dexterity with a needle; the latter a necessary attainment in keeping his kit in good order with no woman (sparing the presence of feminists) to do it for him.[2]

Men *did* actually put little model ships into empty bottles of all shapes and sizes. Some of the most unlikely macho shellbacks were 'dab hands' at embroidery and produced the most delicate things! Painters, sketchers, even a sculptor. One lad was particularly good at drawing an enlargment from a small photograph, then painting-in so that the finished picture looked like an original painting. After a visit to a Spanish bullfight one of the crew had given him a series of action shots developed by one of the Photographers (Fleet Air Arm ratings carried on board at the time) as a favour. Our amateur, untrained artist turned these into a set of very wall-worthy paintings and the ship's carpenter (we had a sailmaker, too!) made up the frames. Some learned an instrument the hard way, by courtesy of a Royal marine bandsman ('Marines first, bandsmen second').

I forgot to mention that we had a surgeon-lieutenant with us who had, as his staff, a petty officer and an ordinary-rated Sick Berth attendant, but the first two soon moved on, leaving only the junior to sit and sleep with us in our mess. 'Doc' ('Call me Gloria') was keen on amateur dramatics and 'Sods' Opera' concerts.

(M. Bree, Leading Writer, HMS *Woolwich* 1949)

Mention of Royal Marine bandsmen reminds me that the carrier I served in carried a Royal Marine band which on ceremonial occasions would be brought topsides by the forrard aircraft lift in the throes of 'A Life on the Ocean Wave', rising slowly into view like Mr Reginald Dixon at the console of his Wurlitzer in Blackpool's Tower Ballroom, a popular turn in the 1950s. Musicians, like many other categories, were in short supply at the time and to maintain the necessary range of instruments, members of the ship's company who could play cornet or euphonium, usually Salvationists, were frequently co-opted. So one might recognize the familiar features of a Chief Engine-room Artificer or a Leading Torpedoman puffing and perspiring under a Royal's white-blancoed solar topee. There was also a bluejacket's pipe band, volunteers – not always Scots for whom there was some excuse – who would render the dogwatches hideous on a crowded messdeck with their chanter-practice. They would on occasion replace the official band in leading the Marine detachment, which was not popular with the Royals as they found the pipes difficult to march behind. Their colour sergeant, who was omniscient as Royal Marine senior NCOs are, or may have previously served with a kilted regiment, advised them: 'The thing to do is get yer bollocks swingin' before you steps off'.

Bandsmen must play at least two instruments, and a big ship's band would also furnish a dance orchestra for the wardroom's entertainment at cocktail parties, both aboard and ashore. This facility was not available for ratings. On 'showing the flag' visits, however, abroad and in home ports, ratings were invariably included in the many invitations from hospitable folks ashore:

If a ship paid an official visit to any port, many invitations would come aboard from all types of people and organizations. For example: '20 chiefs and petty officers are invited to a Darts Match at the WOs and Sergeants' Mess' etc., or '5 officers are invited to a Garden Party' etc. The captain insisted that every invitation was always taken up. In a certain North African port however, an invitation was received for '20 sailors to visit the local prison'. Now naturally no one on board had any interest in that at all so, as had often happened before, 20 ship's company boys were detailed off to visit in the charge of the Padre.

The bus arrived alongside and the Padre herded us boys aboard. The prison gates were opened and the bus drove in; the boys disembarked, with the Padre. Doors in the building opened and out streamed the prisoners – *girls*! Utter chaos, boys being dragged off in all directions, each by two or three prisoners, the Padre running in circles, to no avail. That left just the Padre and myself sitting on the bus, waiting (I always say that for the benefit of my wife). On return aboard news of what had happened spread round the ship and need I add that the list of names under the invitation to 'Visit a local Prison' soon reached the required number.

The thing was, you see, once in prison the 'girls' could only raise money to pay their fines one way – the old-fashioned way.

(J. Leach, Boy Telegraphist, HMS *Superb* 1949)

If this sounds a little like wish-fulfilment, it is the ex-matelot's inalienable right to 'swing the lamp'; a right on which this work relies for much of its colour, if such it has. Here is another excursion which was not quite as planned:

I had just been rated-up ordinary seaman when we called at Funchal, Madeira. A notice went up on the board calling for a dozen or so ratings to sign up for a trip into the hills to a vineyard, invited by the English expatriate owner. We thought this very decent as most invitations in such places were officers only. Anyway, the required number were forthcoming and after dinner on the day we mustered at the gangway in our best white ducks, closely inspected by the officer of the day and warned to be on our best behaviour, like a party of schoolkids on a Sunday school treat. The senior rating, a young and gormless engine-room artificer, was put in charge and handed written orders. We had to report in the first instance to the British Consulate, who were providing transport. We found the Consulate, and parked outside was this magnificent car, complete with chauffeur in chocolate-brown livery. I'm no expert on vintage cars but it might have been a Lagonda, 1920s era. It had woven-cane bodywork, luxurious leather upholstery and gleaming paint and brasswork. It was a huge open car, roomy enough to take all ten or eleven of us.

We set off through the streets, perched up behind our chauffeur like Royalty, with a small Union Jack fluttering from the bonnet. We left the town behind and started to bump over rough, dusty roads. After three or four miles the chauffeur pulled up and asked for our host's address, studying the paper closely, muttering to himself. He drove on another couple of miles before turning off the road through an imposing gateway up a long gravel drive to a big house with a green pantile roof. We dismounted at the front steps and the car drove off. Someone hauled on the bell-pull beside the front door, which after a nervous wait was opened by a Portugese manservant; a small, middle-aged and very dapper man in a starched shirt and grey alpaca jacket. Not a flicker crossed his features as he enquired of us half-score of perspiring sailory our business. Asking us to wait he withdrew, to reappear in a minute or two and bow us inside. We entered a large hallway with oil-paintings on the walls, an elegant staircase and a marble floor. The butler led us into the drawing-room, where we disposed ourselves uneasily in deep armchairs and settees and sat in a heavy silence, broken only by an occasional genteel cough. Jeeves reappeared with a silver tray laden with glasses of very cold beer. We began to relax a little; he assured us that our hostess would join us in a moment, and withdrew.

In no more than a moment Mrs Peek did join us, wearing a welcoming smile and a very fetching cocktail dress of some glazed emerald green material which set off her auburn hair and creamy complexion – she was a stunner. A leading stoker, I think it was, rose to his feet as she entered; collecting ourselves, we hastily followed suit. She motioned us down again and sat among us chatting, quite at ease. Our self-consciousness gradually left us, helped by the beer from our frequently refilled glasses, and we soon got quite animated. Our hostess sipped something from a small glass.

It was only later, over tea and cake, by dint of tactful and seemingly casual questions from our charming hostess, that it gradually emerged that we were in the wrong house. Our intending host, it emerged, was the resident of Peak Lodge, a mile up the road! The chauffeur had misunderstood his instruction. Explanatory phone calls followed, with Mrs Peek, despite her gracious manners, unable to hide her relief. While we waited for a car to take us on to our intended destination, she told us that she had attended a cocktail party for our officers the night before and, she said, had very much enjoyed herself. When her butler announced that several sailors had arrived on her doorstep she was trying to remember, as she dressed, just what she had committed herself to the night before. It said a lot for her poise that she had entertained us lowly matelots with every appearance of enjoying our company, when all the time her mind must have been in a turmoil. Her husband arrived just as we were leaving, and to say he looked surprised would be an understatement – hope he saw the funny side!

In 1962 I was in Funchal on business (with Cable & Wireless) and thought I'd look them up but they had left the island some years before.

(R. Brookes, Ordinary Seaman, HMS *Agincourt* 1950)

There were more 'takers' for liberty when a ship was moored at a jetty and getting ashore was a walk down the gangway, than when at anchor offshore, involving a boat-trip to and from; especially from, in rough weather, on top of steak, egg and chips and several pints of beer, which sometimes proved a calamitous ending to a good run ashore. Though nothing so tragic as what occurred in Portland Harbour on the stormy night of 17 October 1948.

I joined *Implacable* as a Boy in 1947. I was on the *Wrangler* in Rosyth, and they towed the *Implacable* in, put her in a big dock there. We boys were on deck watching – small ship sailors watching this big flat-top come in. I was thinking I wouldn't like to be aboard her, when the coxswain came up, put his hand on my shoulder and said, 'That's your new home!'

They paid-off *Implacable* and a lot of her crew, including me, transferred to *Illustrious*. *Implacable* was beautiful, immaculate, everywhere you looked was clean, spotless. You joined *Illustrious* and she was filthy. It would have taken years of hard work to get her up to *Implacable*'s standard. I think that's what started everybody off – she wasn't exactly a happy ship.

Illustrious was Flag Officer Flying Training and we were down in Portland, swinging round the buoy. One night, the pipe went, 'Away all boats!' and the officer of the watch was saying there were men in the water astern of the ship, and no one really knew what was happening. What had happened was, the pinnace had gone in to pick up the libertymen from Weymouth and had come back in through the breakwater – I think what the problem was, the boat had no canopies on, the canopies had been removed for repainting. It was pretty rough that night, and when they got inside the breakwater it was even rougher. A goffer (large breaking wave) had come in over the bows and everybody piled over to the lee side – she was full-loaded, and over she went. The irony of it was, the MFV (motor fishing vessel) was also in Weymouth, waiting to pick up the chiefs and POs whose liberty ended half an hour later. With hindsight – which is easy enough – they should have hoisted the pinnace inboard that night out of it, because the weather *was* bad. The talk was, that when the Commander was asked if the pinnace could be hoisted, the story goes he said, 'No, it'll teach 'em to be sailors', or something like that. Whether that's true or no, I don't know.

I can't remember how many ended up drowned – quite a few. But of course, I was lucky – I was going to go ashore that night. Somebody came along and asked me if I'd do his duty, and I don't know why – I said yes! So he was in the liberty boat and I wasn't. An AB he was, called Beach. Next morning there was still bodies missing and for two days we in the motor boat were going round all the time, all round the breakwater, and actually we found Beachy. He still had his overcoat on, and the only way we could recognize him was when we cut his overcoat off and he had his name stamped in the back. The crabs had been at him, we couldn't recognize him – he was in the next hammock to me, but I couldn't recognize him. It made me feel funny for a day or two, I can tell you.

We had a memorial service when we'd accounted for everybody, in Weymouth church. Everyone who could be spared went, Marine Band – quite a do. We'd spent most of the previous week guarding bodies, so things weren't very happy on the ship. Then we came back from the church – it was Remembrance Sunday – back to the jetty, and all the next of kin were there. They were waiting, expecting they would be able to go aboard and look round the ship. The skipper wouldn't allow it. Well, when everybody got back aboard there was a lot of chuntering about his insensitivity, and a very bad atmosphere, so much so that the chiefs and POs went along to the Master-at-Arms and said, 'Look, something ought to be done about this because this lot could get out of hand.' So the Jaunty went to see the Commander and said there was trouble brewing and something should be done – we had a lot of Scousers and Scotsmen aboard, and Hostilities Only people, and there was friction with the crew a mix of Devonport and Pompey men – oil and water! She was not a happy ship.

Anyway, the next thing was, the MFV was sent in to bring the people off and that was the end of that episode.

(C. Tonkin, Ordinary Seaman, HMS Illustrious 1948)

Not quite the end. The following report appeared in *The Times* of Thursday, 10 Febraury 1949, headed 'Motor-Pinnace Disaster':

Mr W.J. Edwards, Civil Lord of the Admiralty (Whitechapel, Lab.), made a statement on the disaster to a motor-pinnace containing 51 liberty men from HMS *Illustrious* which was sunk on the night of 17 October last year in Portland harbour with a loss of 29 lives. All the circumstances of this disaster had been thoroughly sifted, he said, by two boards of inquiry, and it had also been possible to raise the pinnace to investigate the cause of its sinking. The immediate causes of the disaster were the overloading of the boat, which should not have contained more than 40 men, and the apparent failure to reduce speed or to turn back to Weymouth pier when the boat encountered rougher water on coming out of the lee of the breakwater and entering Portland harbour. At that point the boat was steered directly into a head sea and foundered when at a distance of only 50 yards from HMS *Illustrious*. With great regret, the Admiralty had reached the conclusion that the responsibility for the accident must be laid at the door of the officer in charge, who unfortunately lost his life. To prevent any misunderstanding owing to the publicity which had been given to this accident, expert examination of the pinnace after raising revealed no defects which could have contributed to the accident. A small leak in the after part of the boat was of trifling consequence. The officer in charge was well aware of it and had caused the boat to be baled out before leaving Weymouth pier.

On the same day, *The Times* published the following, head-lined 'Albert Medal for Young Seaman':

Boy First Class Alfred Raymond Lowe, aged 17, has been awarded the Albert Medal – the *London Gazette* announced last night – for his attempt to save a midshipman when a liberty boat of HMS *Illustrious* overturned and sank in Portland harbour with the loss of 29 lives.

Lowe was trapped under the boat's canopy but struggled clear, swam to a lifebelt, removed his overcoat and shoes, and swam towards the *Illustrious*. When he was under the stern a line was thrown to him. At this moment he heard a cry of 'Help!' and saw that a midshipman about 10 yards away was in great difficulty.

'He grabbed the line and swam to the midshipman, who was unconscious by the time he reached him', *The Gazette* announcement stated.

He endeavoured to turn him over to keep his head above water, but found this impossible and, still holding him, was pulled to the ship's side. A fog buoy was then lowered and he managed to drag the midshipman on to this and to hold on to him until a petty officer came down the rope to assist him. Together they then secured the midshipman, who was then hoisted on board.

The accident took place in eight fathoms of water in a rough sea with a strong wind blowing. Although the midshipman subsequently died, Boy Lowe acted with complete disregard for his own life in leaving his place of safety in an attempt to save him. His action . . . was in accordance with the highest traditions of the Royal Navy.

Alfie Lowe was a classmate of mine at HMS *Ganges* in 1947, a training-ship boy and a very powerful swimmer; the best swimmer in the division and probably in *Ganges*. He was something of a loner then and, according to reports, still is; living in a remote part of New Zealand and sailing his single-handed boat on explorations of the South Sea islands. His action on this occasion was entirely characteristic.

The findings of the official inquiries are in the best tradition of such posthumous investigations; what might be called the 'pilot-error solution' of blaming whoever is safely dead, in this case an eighteen-year-old midshipman. There are some interesting discrepancies between the official account and that of O/S Tonkin, who was there. Tonkin believed the boat's canopies had been removed for painting, yet Alfie's citation said he 'was trapped under the boat's canopy'. Perhaps he was under the midships canopy, which would almost certainly have been left shipped as it protected the engine. Equally, the bow canopy probably was not; if it had been, the 'goffer' which apparently broke over the weather bow, causing men to crowd to leeward and capsize the boat, would hardly have incommoded them. (The reader might be puzzled that the boat should founder on reaching supposed shelter beyond the harbour breakwater. Portland harbour covers a large area, the breakwaters are low, and a strong blow from certain quarters can result in rougher water inside the breakwater, particularly near the harbour entrance, than outside in Weymouth Bay.) The commander's alleged remark on refusing to hoist in the pinnace may be a mere calumny from a disaffected lower deck, though it does have the authentic officer-like ring of contempt; on the other hand, the almost unbelievable lack of human sympathy makes one wonder . . . . In any event, ship's boats should certainly have been hoisted in the conditions prevailing; this is prudent and seaman-like. The MFV, a converted herring drifter, was more than equal to them and could easily have brought off the libertymen. *Illustrious* was still an unhappy ship when I had the misfortune to join her a year later, but at least a lesson had been learned and boats were always hoisted in when the weather got up in exposed anchorages or often not lowered at all, and shore-leave cancelled.

Part of the reason for the discontent on board was undoubtedly the dearth of sports, the ship's demanding flying programme leaving little or no time and opportunity to land teams. Football, hockey, rugger and even cricket had always been a safety-valve for venting Jack's aggression and pent-up energies. Boat-pulling and sailing was rarely indulged in in home waters, whereas in the Mediterranean and Far East fleets the Fleet Regatta was the highlight of the sporting year:

> In the Mediterranean in particular, in the so-called 'years of peace' (when the whole world was going slowly mad around us) rivalry between HM ships and establishments became intense as time for the annual regatta neared – which also included many events like tug-of-war for example which, though not a water-borne sport could be and was indulged in on shipboard and ashore, and there were also the inter-service competitions between the Navy and the other armed services based in the same area. For some reason the boat-pulling races had a very special cachet and there was a special silver trophy in this section much striven for and much-prized if won; much crowed about for ever afterwards by those who actually did the pulling, and by the ship's company of the ship to which they belonged. The silver cockerel would be hoisted to the masthead as a sign of their victory – 'Cock of the Fleet'.
>
> (M. Bree, Leading Writer, HMS *Woolwich* 1949)

This is tongue-in-cheek, even a writer would be well aware that the whole point and purpose of the fleet regatta was to establish which ship was Cock of the Fleet, and provide the excuse for pitched battles in shore-side bars. All branches were expected to provide a boat's crew; there was always a stokers' crew and a cooks' and stewards', pulling against their opposite numbers in the other ships. And for light relief, there included a comic crew of 'odds and sods' dressed in pirate rig, propelling their whaler with carley-float paddles, deck-scrubbers and tin trays. There were other sports to be indulged in, ashore:

> I was initiated in Tangier, as a boy aged seventeen and a half. I think I must have been a lot greener than most at that age even then, though youngsters today wouldn't believe the extent of ignorance among the 'virgin' of both sexes of that era. My oppo Pete Horsley ('Horse') was more experienced than me – which wasn't saying much – as he had a going-steady 'party' at home, and he would relate the details of petting sessions which certainly never went 'all the way', they didn't then. Most of what I heard on the messdeck I simply didn't believe.
>
> Anyway this day was a make-and-mend[3] and boys had leave from 1300, expiring as usual at 1800. I think Pete might have had this particular end in mind, because we soon found ourselves in an Arab-

quarter bar with a brothel upstairs. We had a couple of beers, then Pete approached the 'madam' and disappeared upstairs with her. He reappeared about twenty minutes later, then it was my turn. Well, I won't go into details, but it will give you some idea when I say that I knew I had to wear a rubber, but I thought you unrolled it first and hauled it on like a sock. She was very patient and kind, obviously knowing with what she was dealing – she rolled it up again and applied it as intended, also pushed me off her and rearranged our limbs to make the thing physically possible. I was too excited to be mortified by my comically inept performance and did not trouble her for long.

Incidentally, she must have been familiar with British matelots and their uniform because without being asked she pulled my head down onto her resilient bosom, gripped my jumper and hauled it over my head – sailors' 'tiddley' jumpers were something more than skin-tight and almost impossible to remove without assistance.

(R. Brookes, Boy Seaman, HMS *Agincourt* 1950)

Such inconvenient habiliments were soon to be no longer a handicap:

A feature which came to fruition in the middle/late 50s, was an Admiralty advisory to all commanding officers ashore and afloat, stating that at their discretion, all personnel going ashore may wear civilian clothes. At first, this discretion was greeted less enthusiastically than might have been expected, the reason being that many on the lower deck did not have any suitable clothes to wear, as a number of commanding officers ordained certain modes of civilian dress unacceptable, and so it was with a modicum of relief when many shore-tailors, who for generations had clothed the Navy inside and out regardless of rank, came up with a modified scheme to supply modern up-to-date civilian clothing on the same basis and terms as that for a uniform.

So, relieved of the encumbrances of uniform, as well as its significant tell-tale marker (rating's cap-tally), the matelot came of age and, once clear of the gangway, was able to relax at last. Outwardly now, he was as any other civilian, attracting no attention and able to roam free.

(F. Woods, Leading Stoker, HMS *Contest* 1954)

And that was the end of Jack ashore.

CHAPTER SIX

Crime and Punishment

For a year or two after the war, morale in the Home Fleet was extremely poor. This was partly due to the large number of Hostilities Only ratings awaiting demobilization which, inevitably, was taking longer than those concerned thought reasonable. But at least as much to blame was the apparent ignorance of, or indifference to, the lower deck climate on the part of senior officers who wanted a return to pre-war standards without delay, making no concession to the fact that standards had changed in the postwar world. These factors led to a general breakdown in discipline in some home-based ships, with many cases of wilful disobedience aboard and misbehaviour ashore. Their Lordships' response to this state of affairs was to reorganize and expand the recently-formed Regulating branch, with its new category of Leading Patrolman, equivalent to the army Redcap. Promotion structure was to be to Regulating Petty Officer and ultimately Master-at-Arms, a big ship's senior non-commissioned rank. This was a classic instance of treating the symptom while neglecting the disease.

The first Naval Discipline Act was passed in 1866, codifying offences and punishments. Ninety years later, in 1956, it was revised by a Select Committee to meet modern conditions and requirements: ninety years – almost precipitate by Admiralty standards!

The following passage is from Captain Wells's *The Royal Navy*, quoted earlier:

Notwithstanding increases in pay and improvements to service conditions the post-war unrest left its mark on many ship's companies. As well as petty crime there was persistent leave-breaking to the point where offenders seemed to think there was nothing very wrong in being absent without leave. From 1950 occurred several cases of malicious damage in ships. Steering gear, electric leads and turbines were the principal targets of bloody-minded sailors, some trying to work their tickets. In the aircraft-carrier *Indefatigable*, training young seamen at Portland, Captain R.L. Fisher recollected that in 1953:

'the latter months of the commission were made miserable . . . by some wretch committing sabotage by the devilish method of sticking needles into the multi-core cables. There was latent discontent in the Navy at that time and some of the youngsters imitated him by smashing gauge glasses in the engine rooms. . . . The ship became the permanent home of more than one Admiralty detective and we were constantly harried by press reporters. Appeals by me to chief and petty officers to help find the saboteur produced no response . . . we got him in the end – a Scottish Nationalist electrician.'

[An electrician, naturally. It could hardly have been a seaman, most of whom would not know a multi-core cable from a hammock lashing.]

Reports of incidents were taken up by newspapers who published the complaints about poor food and harsh discipline that did the Navy no credit. In two or three small ships mutual trust broke down to the extent that grave indiscipline followed. After one incident, a Commander-in-Chief reminded the officers of his command that:

'we can none of us feel any complacency about the state of discipline in our ships and establishments unless all of us constantly and consciously take the utmost pains to get to know our men, talk to them off and on duty, study their welfare, respect their pride, commend their well-being and punish their wrong-doing. Perhaps we should use daily King Solomon's prayer for an 'understanding heart to judge our people that we may discern between good and bad'.

A tall order, given that complacency about the lower deck was for many officers a state of mind, and getting to know their men a startlingly novel concept. The phrase 'mutual trust broke down to the extent that grave indiscipline followed' is eerily reminiscent of the inquiry report following the Invergordon mutiny twenty-odd years earlier.[1] And the Commander-in-Chief's liberal entreaties chimed ill with the archaic Naval Discipline Act then still extant, under which at a warship's first commissioning and at set intervals thereafter, lower deck was cleared and sailors stood bare-headed to hear their captain read the Articles of War, with many of the crimes specified therein followed by the awesome formula: '. . . shall suffer death or such other punishment as is hereinafter mentioned'. Of course, for 90 per cent of those crimes the supreme penalty would not, could not, be exacted by this date, but they were chilling words and meant to be intimidating.

Punishments in the Royal Navy were all laid down in *King's/Queen's Regulations and Admiralty Instructions* and in the Naval Discipline Act (and any amendments promulgated). They covered all manner of offences from the very minor to the ultimate (treason, desertion in the face of the enemy, mutiny). The minor punishments were numbered: No. 11, 14, 16 etc. and involved such things as extra work, extra drills etc., having to change into 'rig of the day' and report to the officer of the day at appointed times. Only the very minor 'No. 14' did not also involve stoppage of leave, pay and privileges; the more serious could involve disrating, loss of good conduct badges with their extra pay – even forfeiture of pension. Sentencing to a period of detention in the notorious 'DQs' (detention quarters) was a possibility as too was dismissal from the Service. Civil offences ashore would almost always incur Naval penalty.

As a Writer one of my many duties was to attend at 'Captain's Requestmen and Defaulters' table, supplying all the necessary service documents for the men appearing and any necessary regulations, Admiralty Fleet Orders etc. which the captain might need. I was quite stunned to find that under the Naval Discipline Act the charge sheet for some offences actually contained the phrase: 'is punishable by death, or such punishment as is hereinafter mentioned'. Some punishments, such as flogging, had been substantially reduced after the mid-1850s, to disappear altogether by the turn of the century, but hanging was still on the book. A sobering thought.

(M. Bree, Leading Writer, HMS Woolwich 1949)

The Royal Navy's considerable duty-free privileges were jealously guarded by the wardroom, well aware of the other two services' envy and resentment of them, and severe penalties were meted out to ratings caught smuggling. For a first offence, a senior rating would be disrated, with consequent reduction of pension, and a junior sentenced to a long spell in detention. Among the small library of regulation manuals held by every customs officer was one entitled *Relations with the Navy* – historically, not always cordial[2] – which instructed that the naval offender was to be returned to his ship, and a report sent to his commanding officer. This was after the customs penalty of forfeiture and fine had been exacted, as a civilian would have incurred. Further naval punishment would then be his due. Many customs officers, and particularly the ex-Navy men among them, regarded this double hazard as unjust and would take what measures were open to them to mitigate the offence.

Rum, as mentioned earlier, was a fruitful source of punishment:

Stores were often loaded via a door in the ship's side onto a small flat and up some ladders. The deck at that spot was often covered in dirty oil, fag ends and wood splinters. One day I was part of a loading party when a cask of neat rum was smashed (whether deliberately or not I do not know). Being only seventeen I was shocked to see two older (twenty-one?) ABs go down on their hands and knees and with cupped hands start drinking the rum (with the deck being in the state it was). Later the rum took effect and two hours later they were running around the messdecks with their messmates trying to restrain them. When we all turned to after dinner they tried to hide them from the messdeck Chief who did his rounds then. They were caught and both went to DQs at Pompey.

(C. Taylor, Ordinary Seaman, HMS *Montclare* 1953)

We had an AB in our mess who was a real rum-rat. At 'Hands for rum' he always got at least two tots, his own and a lad's who 'drew' but didn't drink his tot – I don't know if there was any threats involved. He must have been an alcoholic because he could never get enough. One afternoon he got into the motor-boat and smashed the glass of the compass to get at the alcohol the compass-card floated on. He got ninety days' detention for that. He never came back to the ship, I heard he was in RNH with DTs.

(R. Palmer, Ordinary Seaman, HMS *Offa* 1947)

On rating OD (Ordinary Seaman) I was made cell sentry – 3 single cells on board. One night a huge, drunken, black-bearded submariner was brought down struggling and bellowing by *four* sailors. After a struggle they got him into a cell and locked it. I was told, 'When he goes to sleep make sure he does not lay on his back as he might vomit and choke to death.' The submariner was yelling and banging on the door, shouting what he would do to me if I did not let him out. Needless to say I was terrified – the thought of me against him. Eventually he dozed off snoring loudly, with me watching anxiously lest he did indeed choke. Never was I so glad to see my relief.

(C. Taylor, Ordinary Seaman, HMS *Montclare* 1945)

In 1955, newspapers carried a report of a matelot – no doubt trying to get out of the RN and 'working his ticket' – physically attacking a visiting admiral. He was arrested, kicked out of the RN and got 6 months in a civvy prison. Later an OD at Portsmouth barracks when up before the Commodore on a charge tried the same thing – when ordered 'Off Cap', threw it at the officer. Unfortunately for him he was kept in the RN and sentenced to 6 months in DQs.

– Ordinary Seaman Taylor again. For a rating to 'work his ticket' by getting himself repeated stretches in DQs was certainly doing it the hard way, as may be concluded from the following graphic description of what it entailed. Taylor, despite his spell as cell-sentry which might have been expected to put him right off clanging doors and spy-holes, soon became familiar with cell walls from the inside:

He was there when I did 42 days in DQs for leave-breaking. DQs Portsmouth was a three-storey barracks enclosed in very high walls with single rooms (cells). It had a parade ground, separate gym and admin. buildings. The cells had a wooden bench as a bed, a small trestle table and a wooden stool. It was heated by a 'warm' pipe 6in from the floor. There was a strict no-talking rule – so we young men never got to know anyone else's name, rating or what they were in for. Most would have liked to have bragged about why they were in there, but never got the chance – a good ploy by the RN.

Daily routine: called 0600, slop out and visit to heads and washroom. Collected breakfast, ate it at table in cell. Rolled thin mattress and put it outside door. The door placed 6in ajar, waited. NCO shouted, 'Up behind your doors – stand by to jump out – JUMP OUT!' We then jumped out 'at ease' in front of doors. There were about 20 cells each side of a corridor. We then marched off in platoons for a hard physical day, PT or rifle-drill. This was done at the 'quick march' with a rifle movement every time a foot hit the ground, i.e. 'Up – Over – Down' and not 'Up 2, 3 Over 2, 3 Down'. Mini-assault course round the parade ground, where we double-marched round in crocodile fashion – over a 3ft-high wall, water ditch and sand patch. In addition we had 'Rear man to the front!' – he in addition to doubling had to sprint to the front, so there was a constant stream of men sprinting as well as doubling.

Midday break locked up in cells, then more 'instruction' in afternoon and lock-up at 1600. We then had to scrub the table and stool with cold water and wash the floor before 'lights-out' at 2000. Sunday was a quiet day, no drill but church in morning – we had a library book to read that day. In DQs no TV, radio, magazines or newspapers at all.

Food: Breakfast, porridge and kye (cocoa); Dinner, stew and tea; Tea, bread and tea (last meal).

Smoking: As a non-smoker it amused me to see the smokers suffer. Three times a day – breakfast, dinner and tea – we all lined-up and someone went down the line handing out a cigarette to the smokers. Someone then walked along with a light. When he reached the end the 'lighter' went to the front where each smoker had to discard his fag in a tin. This was okay with a lot in the line-up but when there was only 30 or so the smoking-time was much reduced – they had to puff fast to finish the cig.

The 'first-timers' wore khaki gaiters; the 'repeaters', white. The repeaters were given a harder time than the 'firsters'. The Chief Instructor was a 6ft 4in Royal Marine colour sergeant known as 'Tiny', a well-known figure around Pompey.

Despite the severity of this regime, it seemed that Naval detention barracks could no more guarantee to keep determined inmates in, than less-rigorous civilian prisons:

The CPO pensioners who were our Instructors (warders) took pity on three of those who were in for 6 months or more (most of us were 42, 60 or 90 days) and when we were locked up they opened the cells for these three so that they could go and visit each other in their cells (against all regulations I might add). One Boxing Day, Xmas 1955 – they repaid the CPOs by stealing a ladder and escaping over the wall. Of course we could not see out of our cells but just heard running feet and a shout of, 'They have escaped!' Those three and the CPOs were not seen again.

Intrigued by this story, years later I checked the *Portsmouth Evening News* files (January 1956) and read the report which said the three escapees (and named them) had broken into a men's outfitters and stolen clothes; a cafe and consumed several cans of baked beans and two loaves of bread; stolen a motor-bike combination and were arrested near Winchester.

Boys – that is, young ratings aged under seventeen and three-quarters – could not be sentenced to detention, though recalcitrant offenders might undergo cell-punishment within the boys' training barracks. Before that stage, serious or repeated offences earned a caning – the notorious 'cuts' of six or twelve strokes:

I, luckily, never experienced a punishment reserved for Boys, that of 'cuts' – six of the best. I have spoken to boys who underwent it and it convinced me that the powers-that-be did not really consider the actual caning to be the punishment so much as the psychological build-up until the cuts had been administered. I understand the sequence of events were:

  1 Crime committed – stealing or striking a superior etc.;
  2 Officer of the day's Report;

3 Commander's Report;

4 Captain's Report and sentence (2, 3 and 4 above could take longer than a day. Prisoner would be locked in a cell on board);

5 Prisoner given white duck trousers to wear then taken to where the sentence would be carried out. In attendance: doctor, officer of the day, Master-at-Arms, leading patrolman. Prisoner secured to gym horse;

6 Master at Arms requests permission of OOW to apply stroke one;

7 Permission given;

8 Stroke one applied with long cane to prisoner's buttocks;

9 Repeat 6, 7 and 8 above for each stroke until . . . ;

10 All strokes have been applied, MAA then reports this to OOD;

11 Doctor checks prisoner and is either satisfied with prisoner's condition, or not.

I have often wondered how the above sequence of events on a boy of maybe 15, influenced the boy's mind. Did it prevent him from repeating the offence in the future? Did it scar him psychologically? Or would he shrug and get on with his life. I don't necessarily mean the actual cuts, but the long drawn-out build up to them.

If you decide to use this can I suggest you confirm the above with someone with experience of this punishment. As I have said, it is only hearsay.

(J. Leach, Boy Telegraphist, HMS Ganges 1947)

The above account is substantially accurate, though painful as the suspense was, it was as nothing compared to the pain of the cuts.

The great majority of offences were minor ones, with commensurate punishment; crimes such as overstaying leave, being absent from place of duty or slack in turning out of bed in the morning. Such small-time defaulters would be hauled before the officer of the day, being invited by the leading hand or petty officer to 'get your cap and get aft!' The OOD would hear the charge, weigh the evidence cursorily, ask the offender if he had anything to say in answer to the charge and neglect to listen to it. If the offence was such that he could punish it with the limited range of retribution available to him he would do so; otherwise the defaulter would be remanded to 'Commander's Report', where the same procedure would be gone through the next morning. In most cases the offence was absolute and brooked no defence; a defaulter could only offer mitigation, such as the eternal 'OD's excuse', 'I never heard the pipe, sir.' Occasionally a man paraded would have, or at least be convinced that he had, a full answer to the charge. All too often his defence would not be listened to or not believed; some commanders and captains were over-zealous in what they perceived as upholding the authority of petty officers. Such experiences of injustice, or 'naval justice', which to Jack were synonymous, rankled on the lower deck. They, and any other unfairnesses, were known as 'a green rub'.

> We were given a long weekend in 1955 and warned there might be a rail strike. There was – I and my oppo hitch-hiked back on the Monday from the north-east. Tube to Morden, south London and along with hundreds of others started walking back to Portsmouth hoping for a lift. No doubt there were thousands all walking back to their home ports. We got a lift to Petersfield and walked to Waterlooville where we got a bus to the services club near Aggie Weston's where I had a locker. Changed into uniform, had a quick cup of coffee in the crowded restaurant – I did a quick dash to get back on board by 0730. My oppo stayed for a second cup of coffee – along with hundreds of other matelots no doubt. Maybe they thought the Navy would be sympathetic but all the leave breakers – even just a few minutes adrift – were punished.
>
> (C. Taylor, Able Seaman, HMS *Cleopatra* 1955)

Devoid of sympathy, neither were the Regulating branch noted for a sense of humour:

> If you were Home Fleet you would normally get two weeks leave in three months. At Christmas and New Year it was staggered, preference usually being given to Scots for New Year's leave. You had a laid-down amount of travelling-time in addition, done by dividers – as the crow flies. I once asked the Master-at-Arms if he would get me some wings, and he put me in the rattle. (From Chatham to Cleethorpes took longer by train than Chatham to Scotland but they got a day's extra leave because of the actual distance).
>
> (D. Banks, Leading Stoker Mechanic, HMS *Bleasedale* 1949)

Young males do like their sleep, and the easiest way for a green hand to find himself in the daily line-up of defaulters was to be less than prompt in turning out in the morning:

> 'Slack hammock' was not an ineffective method of slinging and lashing our swaying 'leak stoppers'. Probably the first offence most recruits committed was in not getting out of their 'wanking sacks' quickly enough at 'Call the hands'. This reveille took the form of some wide-awake, masochist/moron PO, or lesser mortal duly

appointed, storming through our mess spaces roaring out time-worn exhortations at multi-decibels, originating probably in Nelson's day and lovingly employed and embellished ever since.

'Wakey wakey, rise and shine! The morning's fine and you've 'ad yer time! 'Eave-o, 'eave-o, 'eave-o!, show a leg, show a leg! 'Ands off cocks an' on socks! Look lively now, 'eave-o, eave-o, lash up an' stow!'

And so it would go on, as the rouser shoved and shouldered his weaving way along, accompanied by a solid whack on the underside of a bulging hammock with fist or baton carried by most watchkeepers. This was our 'early morning call'; our alarm clock, our 'braying Chanticleer'. But it was all the warning there would be; should the 'Buffer' (chief bosun's mate), officer or petty officer of the day, quartermaster or anyone else in authority with a nasty turn of mind or a 'weed-on' for some reason, come along to find a body still turned-in – he would soon find himself 'fetching his cap' (meaning being arraigned as a defaulter before the officer of the day for due punishment).

(M. Bree, Leading Writer, HMS *Woolwich* 1949)

Bree goes on to recall a 'green rub' of his own:

I well remember an occasion when some 'gash' had been slung overboard, illegally, through a porthole when I happened to be nominally leading hand of the mess on the day of 'Rounds'. I had been dividing my time between normal duties and looking-in on the mess cleaning; no-one had seen the culprit and no one knew anything of the offence until it was mentioned at the midday meal (a makeshift affair of 'corned dog' and so-called salad, due to the cooks doing their clean-up and hot meals being 'off'). And also all those 'Bluebell'-ed mess traps had to be washed and dried before poisoning all hands. As I was 'in charge' I got the rocket.

Explaining that I had investigated only to find that none of my mess members did it or knew anything of the offence, I was taken over the brow onto the quayside and shown the huge filthy streak of greasy, tea leaf-stained garbage drying in the sun and marring our immaculate paintwork. I was given one hour in which to report back with the name of the culprit. Needless to say I was unable to do so, despite going to the adjoining messes and asking their leading hands at the time. On reporting back without a culprit I was made to go to the bosun's store, draw paintpot and brush, and get a seaman to help me rig a stage over the side and paint over the mess made below our porthole. It was some time later that I discovered the culprit was a bunting-tosser (signalman) from the next mess to ours. He had since moved on anyway, to freedom I think, so I had spent a very hot, unpleasant afternoon working out a punishment for a crime which I, or even my messmates, had not committed in the first place, instead of going ashore as I had intended.

Here we have the classic 'green rub', and an undignified proceeding for any leading hand, particularly perhaps a leading writer. It is unlikely that a leading seaman or leading stoker would have submitted himself to it; a 'culprit' would no doubt have been forthcoming.

Drunkenness has been mentioned as an habitual cause of punishment. Returning aboard from shore-leave 'drunk and incapable' was a common offence, though some officers of the day were more prone than others to turn a blind eye, provided that the inebriated reveller was closely supported by a relatively sober shipmate on either side to keep him upright, and to see him safely struck below. Similarly, coxswains or midshipmen of boats returning to the ship laden with singing, cheering and occasionally vomiting libertymen would be ordered to 'lay off' until order, and quiet, were restored, however long that might take.

Inebriation was not unknown in the wardroom, though much less so than in past years. According to Capt. Wells, 'During the latter half of the nineteenth century . . . heavy drinking by officers, often in private, was widespread. Attacks of delirium tremens were not uncommon, as well as chronic disease of the liver, the worst cases being invalided from the service. When serving as a lieutenant, Prince Louis of Battenburg recollected the stupified bodies of midshipmen being laid out in rows on the flagship's upper deck after a gunroom guest night, each batch marked with chalk so that they could be collected by a boat's crew from their ship.' Small wonder, with such an example from his officers, that the bluejacket of the day 'was unfortunately possessed with the idea that he owed it to his reputation to get outside the greatest amount of drink he could stagger under'. A very few ratings were still possessed of it during our period, but they tended to be older men with hard war-service.

The Navy did have its share of out-and-out alcoholics, but probably no higher a proportion than in many civilian occupations. One I encountered, while serving in a Home Fleet destroyer, was the PO officers' steward – a rating which, no doubt, life insurance actuaries would classify with publicans and barmen ashore, having a similar propensity to helping themselves to the odd tot in passing. The ship was on a cruise to the West Indies and America, lying in Norfolk VA Navy Yard, where the Commander-in-Chief was to transfer his flag from the

Duke of York to us, a shallower-draught ship, to negotiate the Potomac river to Washington DC. The Admiral was to occupy our captain's day cabin, and on this particular day his personal chief steward had repaired aboard with the Commander-in-Chief's private stock of wines and spirits, locking them in the captain's pantry. After lunch the PO steward woozily donned his best shore-going uniform, armed himself with a jemmy, broke open the pantry door and a case of the Admiral's best malt, helped himself to a bottle which he stuffed under his jacket and tottered ashore, proceeding purposefully, if slightly crab-wise, up the quay and out of sight. On return from *his* lunch the chief steward noticed there had been a break-in and informed the Flag Lieutenant, who in turn notified our first lieutenant. The latter appeared to entertain no doubts as to the identity of the culprit and a shore patrol was hastily assembled to locate him and return him to the ship. This they quickly did (the miscreant not having gone far before seating himself wearily on a dockside bollard), but not quickly enough to prevent the last of the malt vanishing down his gullet from the upturned bottle as he saw them approach. The empty bottle was secured as evidence.

This incident served as an object lesson to a young sailor of the awful power of ardent spirit over its slaves, if the example of the messdeck rum-rats was not enough. He just had to have it, whatever the consequences. The consequences were twofold: the PO steward was transferred under close arrest and medical supervision to the flagship and later discharged on medical grounds, and our wardroom officers noticed a marked reduction in their monthly wine bills.

> We had four courts martial whilst in Aden – probably due to the heat and the crowded conditions in which we lived. I remember a Yankee sailor, on being invited aboard *Modeste* for 'sippers', remarking: 'No wonder you guys act like pirates ashore – you sure live like pirates.'
> (A. Zammit, Ordinary Seaman, HMS *Modeste* 1953)

Following the recommendations of the committee set up in 1949 under Mr Justice Pilcher, charged with overhauling the Naval Discipline Act, practice and procedures were brought more in line with civilian courts, including a right of appeal against court-martial findings. Chiefs and petty officers were for the first time given the right to opt for court martial if the charge might involve disrating or dismissal. Otherwise, the captain's summary powers were not interfered with. The original Articles of War had included no fewer than twenty-two offences, ranging from mutiny down to profane language, which carried the death penalty and for ten of them it was mandatory. These were reduced to two or three, again in line with civil law of the time. In practice, according to Hampshire, the last hanging from the yard-arm, Punishment No. 1, took place at Talienwan Bay, China, in 1860, the offender a Royal Marine convicted of trying to murder his captain. The degree of provocation is not recorded.

The committee also wished to abolish the historic preamble to the Act, which referred to 'His Majesty's Navy whereon, under the good providence of God, the wealth, safety and strength of the kingdom chiefly depend', presumably on the grounds of its being no longer strictly true. Unsurprisingly, the Admiralty preferred to retain it and, this being a committee packed with former naval officers, it survived with 'chiefly depend' replaced by 'so much depend'. Soon after the war's end the other two services abolished compulsory church parades, and the Navy had little option but to follow suit. An Admiralty Fleet order dated October 1946 directed that it was to be no longer compulsory for officers and men to attend 'Divine Service performed every Sunday according to the liturgy of the Church of England'. The *Church Times*, reporting the decision, commented: 'In a Service routine, where conduct is organized in every detail, where nearly every act is taken corporately, to make church-going voluntary is tantamount to making it peculiar'. Very true, but as Wells says: 'Divine Service on a voluntary basis continued to be celebrated on Sundays throughout the Navy and if a chaplain was present it was noticeable how his personality and popularity were reflected in the size of his congregation.' This might well have been so – or the size of the congregation could be a reflection of the chaplain's working arrangement with the commander, as in a certain Home fleet aircraft-carrier where the makeshift church in the hangar was usually packed to capacity, especially on cold, wet Sunday mornings when the opters-out were fallen in for Sunday divisions on the flight-deck, standing properly-at-ease in the rain for an hour or more.

It was one of the quainter naval customs to parade requestmen and defaulters together at the weekly Captain's Table, presumably on the principle of: 'We are not just here to punish, you know; bring me your supplications and I will grant them.' An OD relates how he made his routine request to his captain to be rated Able Seaman on reaching the required age and length of service:

As the day approached, the ship's Coxswain, who ran the discipline side of things, told me I would be the last requestman. I think there were two before me, and there was one defaulter, Able Seaman Johnson from the same Mess as myself; charge being drunk and disorderly, fighting, resisting arrest by the shore patrol. A simple matter of doing his best to wreck a bar in Floriana.

On reaching the Captain's table, going through the motions of reports from PO and DO, the Captain looked at me and said, 'If I make you an Able Seaman, will you assure me you will behave like one?'

I couldn't help myself. I glanced over my right shoulder to AB Johnson standing handcuffed to a patrolman, waiting to be sentenced, then looked back to my captain; straight at him, eye to eye, and said 'yes sir, I will'. The eyes started the grin, the DO stared at his shoes, the Captain cleared his throat and said, 'Request granted, rated Able Seaman as of . . .' A good skipper, was Gordon-Lennox.

(R. Grevett, Ordinary Seaman, HMS Mermaid 1952)

Discipline was very strict but you knew exactly where you stood and despite all the hardships the crew had that certain bond and I made shipmates that I'm still in weekly contact with today.

Would I do it all again? Not on your life.

(R. Anderson, Able Seaman, HMS Wild Goose 1953)

CHAPTER SEVEN

Different Ships, Different Cap Ribbons

With the end of the war came an immediate run-down in the number of ships in commission and the closure of many shore bases both at home and overseas. When the dust had settled, the fleet was deployed as follows: the Home Fleet consisting of a single battleship which was the flagship, one aircraft-carrier, one cruiser squadron and two destroyer flotillas. The once huge Mediterranean fleet, pride of the Navy, was reduced to two carriers, a single cruiser squadron and one flotilla of destroyers. In the Pacific, now the fiefdom of the mighty United States Navy, Britannia was represented by a brace of aircraft-carriers, the new capital ships of modern navies, and a handful of cruisers and submarines. The old China station was no more. The gunboats which for years patrolled the Yangtse and West rivers had been withdrawn at the beginning of the war and were not redeployed in deference to the Chinese nationalists, leaving a single guardship at Nanking to evacuate the British Consul-General in case of need.

A British naval presence was maintained in the East Indies with a squadron of cruisers, in the South Atlantic by a squadron based at the Cape, and another on the America and West Indies station. The dockyard at Bermuda was closed down in 1950 and the Freetown base abandoned. At home, the great fleet operational base of two world wars at Scapa Flow in the southern Orkneys was run down, soon to be closed. The separate signal schools at Chatham and Devonport were shut down and all communications training centralized at HMS *Mercury*, East Meon; likewise gunnery schools at the home ports, except for HMS *Cambridge* at Devonport, with training concentrated at Whale Island, HMS *Excellent*. Numerous smaller establishments and stores depots were also closed.

Dictated partly by economic constraints and partly by perceived changes in the Navy's role in the postwar world, a steady rundown in ships, and manpower, was to continue, becoming more or less stabilized by about the mid-1960s. Most of the bloated Reserve Fleet of redundant ships was eventually sold or scrapped. As a result there were far fewer drafts for ratings, particularly to exotic foreign stations – though there were also, of course, fewer bodies to fill the reduced number of billets.

Until August 1954, the same system of manning warships obtained as in the 1920s and 1930s. Ratings on completion of initial training were allocated to one of the three 'Port Divisions' located on the south coast. These were at Devonport (known to Jack as 'Guzz', origin unknown); Portsmouth ('Pompey') and Chatham ('Chats'). Each port division had its own drafting office under the charge of a Drafting Commander and ships as well as men were allocated to one or other of them and manned exclusively by crews based at that port. Thus every warship in commission was either a 'Guzz' or 'Westoe' ship, a Pompey ship or a Chatham ship, and that provenance stamped its character upon it. The advantage for the home-based married rating was that he could make his domestic arrangements, knowing that he would be based at the same port – apart perhaps from absences on training courses, depending on his branch – for the whole of his service. The single men were often less in favour of the system, particularly those whose own homes were distant, as for instance the numerous Scots and Liverpudlians who found themselves at Devonport.

It was at our Part 2 training establishments that the decision was made as to which of the three port divsons (Devonport, Portsmouth, Chatham) we would be allocated and which would henceforth handle all our drafting movements to ships and establishments. Since recruitment, we had been given various 'choices' or invited to 'state your preference' for various things. I use inverted commas purposely, for different circumstances could make a mockery of the words. 'The exigencies of the Service' was as overriding a factor as 'seniority'. To be fair, the Navy did try to allocate, say, a Westcountryman to Devonport as his PD, or a Hampshire man to Portsmouth and a cockney to Chatham – but what to do with a man from Scotland, the north of England, the Midlands? Geographically, the United Kingdom covers quite a small area, but the three port divisions were all on the south coast. Also, the bigger ships with over a thousand in the crew – and there were still quite a few even into the postwar era – mostly divided between Portsmouth and Devonport with not so many at Chatham which was mostly for the small stuff, could not, fairly, be manned from the one Depot which was their home base. There had to be 'seen' to be fairness, at least. Not many sailors relished the 'bullshit' of big ships which could well be carrying an Admiral and his retinue as well as a host of ship's officers, a large regulating branch and a Royal Marine detachment.

Men from all counties had to be fitted into the three Depots' rolls, somehow. There would always be 'cock-ups' in the eyes of the unfortunate sailor who came, perhaps, from John o'Groats and found his port division was Devonport. But the Andrew did try to compensate by allowing such ratings extra travelling time when proceeding to or from leave, for instance. In those postwar years with clapped-out railway rolling stock etc. travel conditions were not of the best and a journey, long-distance, could be fraught with delays, missed connections, late arrivals – and sometimes hard-to-prove explanations on returning 'adrift', which could earn some severe penalties.

(M. Bree, Probationary Writer, HMS *Ceres* 1947)

Each of the depots bore the name of a ship, as did all the Navy's 'stone frigates'; from west to east they were HMSS *Drake, Nelson* and *Pembroke*. When ships of different port divisions operated in company on cruises and exercises, the system bred a (usually) friendly rivalry which heightened efficiency, and enhanced sports' competition.[1] An obvious disadvantage was lack of flexibility. What did not work well was to mix ratings of different port divisions in one ship's company, as operational necessity sometimes dictated (a good example of this was *Illustrious* – see page 70). But such intermixing had had to be done during the war when the port division scheme proved, for a variety of reasons, impossible to maintain. As it was clearly not a good idea to operate a system in peacetime which was unsuited to war conditions, their Lordships were considering alternatives. From August 1954 they reduced the length of foreign commissions in response to the general feeling that in the current climate two and a half years' unaccompanied service overseas was too long a separation for married men. More to the point, it was making it difficult to retain senior ratings; most of whom were, of course, married. Foreign service afloat was henceforth reduced to a maximum of eighteen months from leaving UK to return.

Before the war and for a couple of years afterwards it was usual, at least for the bigger warships, to commission for foreign service in their home ports and steam out to their stations, where they would relieve a ship due to return home. (I recall seeing the cruiser *Euryalus* in Devonport dockyard, looking very tiddley in her pale grey Mediterranean paintwork, preparing for departure. She lay alongside with slackened mooring lines with her entire ship's company rushing from side to side of her upper deck. This was the Navy's somewhat elementary tilt test). Passage-time out and back excluded the two and a half years on station and could add, in the case of a Far East commission, ten or twelve weeks to the time away.

Even where a ship was recommissioned on station, the new ship's company was transported out and the old one home in the detested troop-ships, in which below-deck conditions were so bad that on more than one occasion servicemen granted shore leave at ports en route refused to return aboard without promised improvements. This again was where the authorities were exceeding slow to grasp that men in all three services were disinclined to put up with conditions in peacetime which were accepted as a matter of course during hostilities. Troop-decks were less of a culture shock to sailors who were used to similar conditions and made the best of things than to soldiers and particularly airmen, who weren't.

With the shorter foreign commissions making time of the essence, and the Admiralty's acceptance that flying-machines had a future, it was decided to leave virtually all ships on station and to relieve them by air. The early days of air-trooping were brimming with novel departures:

We were one of the first ship's companies to fly out to Singapore, in September 1954, to recommission *St Brides Bay*. This was my second Far East draft, having done nearly two years on *Kenya*, '48 to '49. What a difference! When it began, trooping flights were done by civilian airlines on charter, the reason for this was that India, I think it was, had a strong neutrality policy (cold war and all that) and would not allow military flights to cross its airspace. So there had to be this fiction – which I'm sure the Indian government knew all about but which enabled them to deny it – that we were civilians!

We had a briefing at RNB and were issued with civilian passports. Then we were trained to London and reported to Goodge Street Deep Shelter, next to Goodge St Tube station, which was I believe a stretch of Tube railway built but never used as such, and was a deep air-raid shelter during the war and now a trooping embarkation centre. The entrance was well-concealed in a yard with a small brick guardroom staffed with Crushers.[2] In the middle of the yard was a dome-like structure in which was a lift and the top of a very long spiral staircase of about two hundred concrete steps. Officers only could use the lift both ways but other ranks only up; we had to take the staircase down, humping kitbags and hammocks. The shelter was staffed by the Army, RASC or RAOC, the 'blanket-bashers'. Down below it was a hive of activity – plywood-walled stores and offices and two-tier wooden bunks built along both walls of the tunnel. Also kitchens and eating-areas, it was all self-contained.

After a meal which I can't recall – it must have been so bad that memory has blotted it out – we were led to a storeroom where the squaddies issued us all with identical two-piece, single-breasted grey flannel suits, a cream-coloured shirt and a tie (various patterns) for which we had to sign. The suits were in a range of sizes and most of us got a reasonable fit. Then we turned in, and after a restless night and a long queue to wash and shave in the morning – they said it was morning, it could have been any time down there – we donned this rig and had breakfast. The squaddies took charge of our kitbags and hammocks – we had been issued with a list of kit to carry with us in our pusser's grips – we went up in the lift in batches of ten and assembled in the yard. It was good to see daylight again.

After half an hour's wait an airline bus arrived – it was pale blue and white with 'Skyways' painted in dark blue down the sides and it had a kind of extra half-deck on the top; this was the 1950s when air-travel was still glamorous. I think the buzz was that we were going to Northolt but we ended up at Stansted after about an hour's ride. This was still pretty much as it had been when an American air force bomber base, the terminal buildings were Nissen huts with bits built on. We queued up at the reception desk like normal passengers, which is what we were as far as the airline was concerned, and was each given a civilian flight ticket. The uniformed girls addressed us as 'Mr' and were very polite! It must have been about 1100 by this time. There was still an hour to take off and we were ushered into a cafe area and served eggs and bacon!

Fortified by this unexpected repast it was still something of a shock when we got out on the tarmac and saw our waiting aircraft. The fresh 'Skyways' livery couldn't hide the fact that it was a converted wartime Lancaster bomber, this conversion was called a 'York' and there were several in service with the charter companies which sprung up after the war. We had seen the crew board ahead of us – two pilots, navigator or radio officer and three attractive hostesses in neat uniforms. The senior pilot had a big handle-bar moustache and a chestful of medal ribbons – it occurred to me he might have flown this same plane before, with a bomb load.

For most of us this was our first flight – and what a flight! The vibration was terrific and the engine-noise deafening, so much so that you had to bellow in the ear of your neighbour in the next seat to be heard, we soon gave up trying to converse. The flight out to Singapore took four days. We were treated very well by the crew – spoiled, by our standards – the same treatment as their normal customers got, no doubt. I don't recall any meals on the plane, I think coffee and beer was served, because the York's range being so short we had to keep landing to refuel and had most of our meals on the ground. I remember we landed at Rome, Malta (night-stop), Bahrain, Karachi (night-stop), New Delhi, Calcutta (night-stop), Bangkok and Singapore. We were put up in the best hotels – unbelievable treatment for matelots! Our last night-stop was at the Great Eastern hotel, famous in the Raj days, where we dined in state with turbanned bearers serving the food from silver dishes and hovering behind your chair to refill your glass (with water!). Like a Hollywood film. It was there that, as we arrived and went up the huge marble staircase from the foyer, thirty-odd of us all identically dressed, we passed on the stairs two regular guests and I heard one say to the other, 'Who is it – the Moscow Dynamos?'[3]

We arrived at Singapore late on the fourth day after leaving UK and were bussed to HMS *Terror*, the naval base, where we came down to earth in more ways than one! Next morning we handed in our civvy suits, cleaned into working rig and went down to the ship, where the two flights ahead of us were already installed, and so began the commission.

Just to round this off – we flew home in February 1956, still by civilian airline but 'Airwork' this time and the aircraft was a Hermes, a bit more up-to-date than the York, but not a plane with a very good safety record. In fact only the previous week a Hermes had crashed on take-off at Malta or Cyprus with a full load of squaddies, most or all having been killed. It didn't do anything for our confidence when, having been told of a slight delay due to technical problems the 'Airworks' local agent, who had met us on arrival in a crisp white tropical suit, appeared in the departure lounge with rolled-up shirtsleeves and his hands and arms covered in oil up to the elbows and announced, 'I think she's OK now!' She was, and we only took three days to get home, landing at Heathrow when Terminal Two was still wooden huts and duckboards.

(J. Christison, Leading Seaman, HMS *St Brides Bay* 1954)

For the first few years, trooping by air continued to be performed by civilian airlines on charter but was eventually allocated to the RAF and their fleet of Hercules troop-carriers – safer flying perhaps, but less exciting.

Under the existing system of drafting from base ports, RNB or 'Depot' loomed large in a rating's service life. This was because he would normally pass through barracks between spells of sea service or when landed for a training course. Depot was a kind of periodic check on ratings; 'joining routine' involved visits to doctor, dentist, pay office, gas chamber, 'clothing class' for kit-muster and many more, being sure to get from each an authenticating rubber-stamp on his 'joining card'. Drafting routine involved the same round of visits, even if the two events were only a week apart. As described in Chapter 3, sailors were put to 'gainful' employment in the Depot Working Party (DWP), or 'Slave Market' once joining routine was completed, so the old salts among them contrived to stretch it out for several days. Like any vast, impersonal service establishment, the thing to do to avoid the attention of the Gestapo, or Barrack Guard, was to move purposefully from place to place, carrying a joining card or something which looked like a joining card. When inevitably, the sailor ran out of dodges and was conscripted into the DWP and given his demeaning armband to wear, his name and ship's book number entered in the barrack rolls, his soul was no longer his own. Failure to muster for the morning Slave Market in the drill shed would within minutes have the Gestapo on his track, and once detailed for a working party, his station card – his 'licence to breathe' was taken from him until 'Secure' was sounded at 1600 hours.

Then on to HMS *Drake*, Royal Naval Barracks Devonport. A proper stone frigate. Accommodation consisted of a large room on the first floor, very sparsely furnished with old leather settees and armchairs, a few tables and chairs, insufficient lockers and hammock billets. Coal-burning stoves supplied what little heat there was, more often than not there was no vacant space around them. Meals were taken in a vast dining hall on the second floor, and a meal-ticket had to be produced. But the meals were good.

After Divisions in the morning, as stokers we would invariably be on a coaling party. This meant going to the coaling depot, filling sacks and loading them on low trucks towed by a 'Lister' which was then driven by a civilian to all the boiler rooms in the barracks where they were unloaded and tipped. If lucky, at 'Stand easy' a cup of tea and biscuits could be purchased at the NAAFI. But if away from the NAAFI building, a 10-minute smoke break had to do.

At the end of a working day it was always a rush to the bathroom, which was in a basement under the main block. The bathroom consisted of about a dozen cubicles with a cold-water fitted bath and no door, only a doorway. Hot water had to be fetched in buckets from a boiler. This ran cold after a few bucketsful so a tepid bath might be obtained if lucky. More often than not it was a cold-water sluice before going to the evening meal. That is if you could get a bath cubicle and put water in it before someone else pinched it. Altogether a very bad state of affairs. After which you might be duty watch, which could mean anything from fire party to sentry. The regulating branch never did this as usually they stood back and took the credit whilst others did the dirty work.

(K. Moore, Stoker Mechanic, HMS Drake 1950)

It was all too typical of the Royal Navy of the day that men who had spent seven or eight hours coal-hauling were left to shift for themselves without hot water to bathe in. Where were the stokers' divisional officers, apart from enjoying tea and toast in the wardroom; and did they even know of the situation? Probably not; officers had very little contact with ratings in RNB, that impersonal place with a transient population of thousands. Surprisingly, most ex-matelots have pleasant memories of the food in RNB – at least in Jago's – though that may say more about the standard of victuals on board ship than in Depot:

> Some of my lasting impressions of 'Jago's Mansions', as so often in those days of rationing and shortages, concerned 'food, glorious food' in comparison with that of the training days. In particular I recall – as many will – the thick pea soup served up in the big aluminium cans; one can to an 8-seater table, together with a plate of thick crusty bread baked on the premises in the bakeries behind the mess hall. For some reason I found many just did not seem to like this thick green ambrosia and I have sat and eaten (drunk would be inappropriate – one couldn't drink this, it was far too solid) plate after plate until I had to stop in order to leave room for a couple of slices of bread and jam with which to finish supper, the meal at which it was usually served when we worked late.
>
> Always, but *always* did 'Jago' have bottles of brown sauce on the tables; not the sauces most people know today and the TV screens plug; this was a sauce, in my opinion – and that of others – which surpassed all other bottled sauces, but I've never found it anywhere else or met anyone not ex-Devonport barracks who has ever heard of it! I refer to 'Ally Sloper's', in a large glass bottle with a gracefully tapered neck. The label bore a picture depicting a cheeky-looking gent wearing a tall hat of some sort. I forget the actual picture but the slogan 'PUT PLENTY ON!' was printed across the top somewhere. Good advice! It was a great sauce and though I've never tasted it since last leaving 'Jago's' to go for my demob suit, I can almost taste its fruity spiciness as I write this.

(M. Bree, Writer, HMS Drake 1950)

Nothing has been heard from the rating occupying the adjacent hammock billet to Writer Bree.

There was a 'ticket' of some sort to regulate almost every aspect of a rating's life in Depot: the station-card to keep him at work and allow him to go ashore; the meal-ticket with its dated sections and a similar one to draw his rum ration.

Myself and another leading hand were told off as 'mess caterers' for one of the barrack rooms. We occupied a small open-topped 'caboose' at the end near the stairs, with a two-tier bunk instead of hammocks and a couple of wooden lockers. (Incidentally, this caboose was infested with fleas. I don't think I had ever had a flea-bite before in my life, and I woke the first morning covered with them, as was my oppo. We had to buy flea-powder ashore and dust everything down.) Our duties were not too strenuous and were as follows: every morning at 0800 we reported to the regulating office and got a daily list of all drafts in and out to update the nominal list for our mess. Then we went to the mail office to collect the post and distribute it, also re-direct any for bodies who had left on draft (this nearly all consisted of football-pool coupons, for which there was no chance of reaching the body in time to enter, so they usually ended up in the gash-bin). This done, during the morning we supervised the hands detailed off as room sweepers. Now comes the interesting bit:

At 1130 we had to go to the spirit room to escort the handcart with the day's rum issue loaded on it, down to the drill shed, where at 1145 it was dished-out. The grog was mixed using a water tap in a corner of the drill shed. It was then dished out from fannies on trestle tables set up with the mess number prominently displayed on each. Ratings queued up at the appropriate table for their grog, issued by the mess caterers, supervised by the officer of the day who was usually a commissioned boatswain or gunner. The rating handed his rum ticket to one caterer who clipped off the day's date with a kind of hand-punch, while the other caterer measured out a tot to the rating, who had to drink it down there and then – this was to prevent hoarding. There were several hundred men drawing their tot – the queues never seemed to get any shorter and the issue took nearly an hour. Obviously with that quantity of grog there was going to be plenty over, as a generous 'plussers' was always added – it was never known exactly how many bodies would be 'drawing' on a given day, with so many comings and goings. Any surplus went down the drain under the tap.

On our first day my oppo, whose name was Gooch, and I realized that the OOW wasn't paying much attention – at least he couldn't see us where we were with all the bodies milling about; there were several tables, all with queues. So it wasn't difficult for us to make a big show of pretending to clip each other's tickets and down a tot. In the course of an hour I downed three, and I don't know how many Goochie had. After the issue we went for our dinner – I was feeling no pain, but we were OK, or so I thought until I heard a thud and splash and Goochie's head was in his soup. I got a couple of lads to help me up the stairs with him and get him turned in – fortunately we weren't seen. It would have been disrating and probably cells. We never repeated it – moderation in all things!

(G. Curtis, Leading Seaman, HMS *Drake* 1951)

Very often a rating would find himself in RNB for an indeterminate period; typically, he would have left his previous ship at the end of its commission and would languish in barracks until a requirement arose for his particular branch and rating elsewhere, when his name and number would surface in 'Drafty's' records and he would receive a summons to the Drafting Office for orders. He had no choice in the matter of where – or when. Married ratings with rented local accommodation (natives) might be given sufficient notice of a draft to rearrange their affairs, though there was no guarantee, and many a wife was left to pack up and go to mother's. Single men got long enough, usually, to complete the draft routine referred to earlier. But this was not always the case:

I got a pierhead jump from Guzz barracks in October 1949. A real green rub. I had just finished 18 months on *Duncansby Head* in the Reserve Fleet and I was hoping to get on a course for Leading Signalman. I had only been in Depot about three days; I was in the NAAFI at 'stand easy' when the tannoy sounded off – 'Signalman McIntyre report to the drafting office, at the double!' – it was quite a shock hearing my name blaring out like that, and of course I didn't like the sound of the message! I got to the drafting office and knocked on the sliding hatch. It shot back and some red-faced old b****** of a three-badge PO said 'What do you want?' I told him and he made some sarcastic remark about me taking my time (I didn't double all the way, it was about half a mile), took my station card off me and slapped a draft-chit down on the counter. 'You're going to the *Cumberland*, he said. 'Clean into number twos, get your kitbag and hammock and get yourself down to the pierhead, chop chop.'

I must have been staring at him gobsmacked, and he said, 'What are you waiting for, laddie? Get a wriggle on, she's just come in and she's sailing again right away, if you're adrift you're in big trouble, right – away you go!'

I just had time to get down to the mess, empty my locker into my kitbag, and with the kind help of an AB who was on a loaf from a working party and who carried my 'mick' for me, get down to the pierhead to catch the boat sent to collect me from *Cumberland* which was anchored out in the Sound. She was the Navy's 'floating laboratory' at that time, testing new weapons and various gadgets. This was a real 'pierhead jump' for me – literally! I soon found out that I was replacing a bunting-tosser who had just been landed to Stonehouse[4] with TB. I did ten months aboard her, then managed to get a draft direct to *Mercury* for my killick's course,[5] so escaped another spell in *Jago*'s, much to my relief – I never had good memories of that place.

(J. McIntyre, Signalman, HMS *Drake* 1949)

Joining a ship, even a big ship, involved much less formal rigmarole than joining RNB:

A rating joining a ship from RNB would report his arrival to the officer of the day and usually be directed to the head of his particular department to be allocated his berth. There, he would contact his senior rate of the mess to be shown his locker, sleeping billet etc. and his working part of ship. In a small ship, say a destroyer or frigate, the locker would consist of a small steel box construction into which he had to pack all his kit and wordly goods. The leading hand of the mess would then enter the rating's name on a roster for various mess duties. After which he would be shown his working part of ship and given an opportunity to look around and familiarize himself accordingly.

(F. Woods, Leading Stoker, HMS *Contest* 1951)

Contest was a destroyer, and Leading Stoker Woods would soon have settled in, especially if he had served in a similar ship previously. It was a different matter when, for instance a small-ship sailor found himself lost and disorientated, aboard an aircraft-carrier. He would feel himself confined in a huge labyrinthine steel prison, required to find his way about the ship to attend his place of duty and various musters which demanded his presence. For the first few weeks he would be constantly getting lost, climbing up and down accommodation ladders and wandering alleyways until something looked familiar; he could hardly ask directions without bringing upon himself derision and contempt. In those early days he would frequently be adrift for watches and musters and, to begin with, might be allowed to plead getting lost as an excuse. Lest this should be counted an exaggeration, here are the observations of an old sea-dog, a merchant navy master mariner who might be assumed to be familiar enough with the insides of big ships. In March 1950 he spent a week aboard a fleet carrier as a guest of her captain to gather material for a book. He records: 'After lunch on this first day . . . I explored the fantastic maze of the great ship's interior. Without a dexterous guide I must have lost all orientation, all ideas of direction. Water-tight compartments, intricate alley-ways, steaming washrooms, odoriferous galleys – the ship was a mobile city, and as baffling as old-time Babylon must have been.[6]

In a ship of this size, with a complement of 1200 or more, many crew-members would still be unfamiliar with, and capable of getting lost in, vast tracts of it which were not on their daily round, so to speak; it is likely that the old gentleman's 'dexterous guide' was a member of the regulating staff, or the fire-fighting and damage control team.

Naturally, the longer and more varied a rating's service, the more adaptable and less prone to be flummoxed he would become. The following is fairly typical of a naval career of medium length:

I joined the RN on 4 January 1949 (actually travelled to join HMS *Ganges*, Shotley on my 15th birthday) as a Boy Second Class, becoming during training a Boy First Class and a Boy Telegraphist before joining my first ship, the Battle class destroyer HMS *Corunna* in May 1950. During my time aboard her I became an Ordinary Telegraphist, seeing service in UK and Mediterranean Waters, then as a Telegraphist. Following this, I got a shore draft to South Africa, Capetown/Simonstown Radio, being ashore from May 1952 to September 1954 when I returned to UK.

Later that year I was drafted to an inshore minesweeper, HMS *Burley*, running from Port Edgar on the Firth of Forth. In January 1955 I was sent to HMS *Mercury*, Leydene, Portsmouth and transferred to the then Radio Warfare Branch, making Leading Telegraphist (Specialist) and then Petty Officer Telegraphist (S) before leaving the RN on 2 January 1961. During the intervening years I had drafts of varying length ranging from a few days to a couple of years, aboard HM ships *Pickle, Boxer, Euryalus, Apollo, Lynx, Leopard, Turpin, Royal Charlotte* and *Afrikander* (South Africa again). The ships ranged from fleet minesweepers to cruisers, from frigates to destroyers, from mine-layer to submarine and of course, shore establishments and bases in UK and overseas. So I guess I experienced a whole gamut of living conditions both as the lowest rating to 'middle-management' as a Petty Officer.

(G. Bullock, Petty Officer Telegraphist, HMS *Turpin* 1950)

On promotion to petty officer, a rating enjoyed a marked improvement in his living conditions, including the services of a messman to prepare and serve his meals and clean his accommodation in an 'enclosed' mess. He was also entitled to the messman's assistance in conveying his baggage when he went on draft, unlike the junior rating who humped his own:

> To transport one's allotted burden of kit, together with the personal lumber one always collected, was – the 'Handcart, naval, wooden, wheels iron-shod, painted crab-fat (Admiralty grey)'. Those old enough to have had an old-fashioned 'trek cart' in their Scout troop will know roughly what the thing looked like, but these monstrosities were much bigger and heavier! For a rough idea, imagine something like the horse-drawn flat wooden cart that had two long shafts for the horse and low boards at the sides. This cart had, not two shafts, but a single central flattish beam, fitted at its outer end with a large, worn-shiny T-handle. Lord knows how many pairs of horny hands had shoved those damned contraptions over the cobbles of RN dockyards.
>
> Huge as the thing was it was never big enough to take all one's gear without something falling off – one hammock, with wafer-thin mattress/palliasse; one canvas kitbag; one large, green-canvas issue suitcase; one smaller, brown fibre 'weekend' case; one respirator, and whatever else necessary, or possessed.
>
> (M. Bree, Writer, HMS *Drake* 1950)

Writer Bree, together with handcart, joins his first ship:

> Dropping the cart at the foot of the brow I ran smartly up it, saluted the quarterdeck (obligatory, even a 'quarterdeck' on a shore base!) and turned to look for wherever the quartermaster was lurking. Explained I was joining the ship and who I was etc., and he directed me down the nearest upper deck hatch. I followed his directions to the Regulating Office where I reported again, this time to the Master-at-Arms (known as the 'Jaunty' or 'Jossman') and he took me across several flats (lower deck spaces) aft to the officers' cabins. I was there introduced to a Lieutenant (S) who was to be my divisional officer. The '(S)' denoted an officer of the Supply and Secretariat branch, responsible for all food, clothing, rum, tobacco etc., and all secretarial, record-keeping and pay, and the serving of all meals in

galleys and wardroom. All these are the province, respectively, of Writers, Stores Assistants, Cooks, Officers' Cooks and Wardroom Stewards.

A most unusual draft which fell to the lot of a very few sailors was that which came the way of Leading Electrician, Gordon Jay, he of the mishap with the paint-pot, in 1954:

After this I was drafted to HMS *Delight*, a new destroyer building at Fairfield's shipyard on the Clyde. We were standing by the ship while she was fitting-out. It was during this period that an AFO came out asking for volunteers for the new Royal Yacht's permanent crew. It sounded very interesting and certainly preferable to the misery of my Clydebank 'digs' so I put my name forward.

After a few weeks I was called to attend an interview at Chatham barracks. This I duly did, and afterwards returned to Glasgow to carry on with fitting out *Delight* and maker's sea trials. Following successful (eventually) completion of the trials, I was sent for one day by my divisional officer and told I had been successful and was to join RNB Portsmouth for kitting out with *Britannia's* uniform.[7] This came as quite a surprise because applicants had been flown home from overseas for interview and competition was hot.

Be that as it may, I very soon found myself back in Glasgow, in fresh digs, standing by *Britannia* in John Brown's yard on the other side of Clydebank from Fairfields. Thus began a wonderful spell of service as a 'Yachtie' in those early days, when the whole crew was permanent. We were all proud to be on that superb ship, and all reference to normal working hours and ship's routine went out the porthole . . . I cannot breach the rules of confidentiality while on board *Britannia*. Suffice it to say that it was fascinating, exciting and indeed educational, which I terminated reluctantly when my promotion to Petty Officer came through.

Rules of confidentiality notwithstanding, it is known that many Royal Yacht crewmen of long service formed quite close, informal relationships with members of the Royal Family, particularly the children, to whom some of them acted as 'minders' on board, or nannies. The royals were at their most relaxed when aboard the yacht and formality was at a minimum. Royal yachtsmen were known by their first names or nicknames whilst aboard. There was a distinct cachet to being a member of *Britannia's* crew, as ratings found when they were endlessly feted during the yacht's visits to foreign ports.

Of course there was a down side. It was inconceivable that any of those card-carrying, leftward-leaning electrician's mates could have filtered through the meticulous crew selection procedures – which was just as well, given the stark contrast between the splendours aft and the crew accommodation. A former crew member from 1961 to 1968, ex-Stoker Mechanic Tony Grimmer, relates in an article in the commemorative 'Farewell Britannia', published by *Navy News*: 'There were eight bunks for 24 blokes. It has been said that pigs in a sty had more room to live in. As the newest recruit, I was taken to the engineering workshop and ordered to sling my hammock above a lathe. If any work had to be done on the lathe during the night, I was rudely awakened.'

The article goes on: 'Tony graduated to a camp bed between two sewage tanks, then moved to a passageway and only gained a bunk in the last eight months of his service.' But he looks back happily on his royal yacht service adding: 'I was on the greatest ship afloat, being paid to see the world. The camaraderie was magnificent and there was tremendous pride in the ship.' If there was any 'yachtie' who did *not* enjoy and take great pride in his service, he is yet to testify.

The shorter commission introduced in 1954 was followed three years later by a shorter continuous-service (CS) engagement of nine years. For many years the CS engagement was twelve years from the age of eighteen for a boy enlisting at fifteen, i.e. up to fifteen years in total. Adult recruits could however opt for 'Seven and Five' – seven years regular service plus five years on the Reserve – allowing them to return to civilian life while still young enough to begin a new occupation. On completion of the initial twelve a rating could 'sign on' for a further ten years to pension at age forty. Later, with a continuing shortage of senior rates, selected men could extend their service by a further five years. This was known as the 'Fifth Five', or in the vernacular, 'Fifth Prick'.

For time out of mind, the matelot's favourite entreaty, frequently voiced at moments of stress and frustration, was: 'Roll on my *****twelve!' Presumably this became 'Roll on my ***** nine!'; less distant but no more imaginable, at the time.

That same year, the century-old port division system was abolished. Henceforth all drafting was centralized in a single drafting office initially located at Haslemere, with the ship-name HMS *Centurion* and a Drafting Commodore in command. *Centurion* was subsequently moved to Gosport to be nearer the heart of naval affairs.

Two and a half years was the standard foreign commission. No cheap fares, no married quarters; sometimes you were away three years in the Far East. I walked into Devonport Barracks straight from training, received foreign service draft leave of 14 days which meant they could send you anywhere without leave instantly. I was 16 when I was sent to *Euryalus*, the youngest in the engine-room. I was 19 when I returned, but then I was single. What must it have been for married men. I know that many marriages didn't survive. I wonder if the New Navy would put up with that? I don't know what they mean when the brass use the term 'New Navy' – do you?

(B. Whitworth, Stoker Mechanic, HMS *Euryalus* 1950)

CHAPTER EIGHT

Classes for Instruction Fall In!

The primary function of an armed service in peacetime is to prepare for war. In this respect, the postwar Royal Navy did its best in a period of economic restrictions to adjust to its new, subordinate, role in NATO and cope with the difficulties caused by a shortage of key senior ratings. It was however, a good time for an ambitious junior, who would generally receive every encouragement to get on. This was in marked contrast to pre-war when promotion was slow and a duly qualified man could wait years for a vacancy in the next higher rating: promotion rosters in most branches were 'dry' – that is to say, empty – and rating-up came in the time it took papers to be processed. Compared to the dearth of 'sea-time' in home waters, with exercises and evolutions for the most part confined to the much-depleted Home Fleet's semi-annual cruises in spring and autumn, the Navy's shore-based training effort was prodigious and diverse.

Most new recruits ('nozzers') underwent a common syllabus of basic (Part One) training, though in the early postwar years the various branches still ran their own separate new-entry establishments.[1] Part Two training, usually at a different establishment, consisted of the elements of 'technical' grounding in their branch: seaman, stoker, supply and secretariat, cook, steward, sick berth attendant. Other recruit specialisms, such as electrical, were to come later. Artificer apprentices who entered by competitive examination at the same age as boys, and trained for four years ashore before drafting to sea as Artificer Fifth Class with acting petty officer rate, were a special case.

Basic training, as in all armed services, was designed to be rigorous, with 'breaking-in' its primary aim. Add to this the Royal Navy's penchant for archaic, age-of-Nelson attitudes to discipline and living conditions, and the following experience was all too drearily familiar:

On completing my part one training at HMS *Excaliber*, I was drafted to HMS *Imperieuse* for my stoker training. This was probably the most hated ship in the Navy at that time and was in fact the old battleships *Valiant* and *Revenge* tied up alongside each other in midstream about a mile up from the dockyard. For reasons best known to the Admiralty we were treated like animals. The food was almost starvation diet supplemented by a third of a loaf per man per day but with an extra diet of as many cockroaches as you could eat, the ship being infested with them.

Punishment was given for the slightest thing and was usually 'Number Eleven' – doubling for long periods with your rifle held above your head and was continued until some ratings collapsed. I once saw one rating who was so distressed that he jumped overboard rifle and all and struck out for Torpoint, which was over half a mile away. Fortunately a boat was launched and he was picked up and brought back on board, but he was put on a charge and was back on Number Eleven the next day. The officers seem to have been picked for their cruelty and I never saw them show any mercy when they took defaulters for punishment. I recall one CPO who would hit us with a rope's-end if our rifles were not held high enough when doubling. I and many others always vowed what we would do to him if we ever met up outside.

Without doubt the worst officer was a Lt. Franks who seemed to take great pleasure in sending men back for the slightest thing when they fell in to catch the liberty boat, e.g. a speck of dirt on your boots, lanyard looks dirty, hair-cut; but his favourite was, 'You need a shave' – in most cases to fresh-faced young lads who had never shaved before and only had a bit of bum fluff on their chins.

Reveille was at 0600 and we were given ten minutes to stow hammocks and report on deck in bare feet to scrub the decks with salt water, it was my misfortune to have been doing my training in the middle of that severe winter. There were so many things aboard this ship that made our lives a misery, but the one highlight to our week was when we got paid and went to the canteen where the NAAFI manager made a bomb selling us slices of fruit cake.

Perhaps the only good thing out of the *Imperieuse* was that for the next seven years hardly any part of my later Naval service was as bad.
(D. Goodall, Stoker Mechanic, HMS *Imperieuse* 1947)

At a time when recruitment was a serious problem for the Navy, to treat much-needed new entrants to the engine-room branch – young men who would be going home on leave to tell their mates what a grand life it was – so unnecessarily harshly, seems crass beyond belief.

A stoker, later to be called Stoker Mechanic and later still, Engineering Mechanic (a rose by any other name . . .), in common with most other branches, gained advancement by taking a training course and passing an examination for the next higher rate. Seamen were somewhat different as they, like their officers at that time, were required to specialize. In addition to taking courses and passing examinations for leading seaman and petty officer known as 'seamanship boards' – their 'substantive' rate – they would also, as young ordinary seamen have chosen, or been selected for, specialization in one of the categories which had proliferated during the war. These were gunnery, torpedoes, anti-submarine (Asdic, later sonar), radar plot plus the more obscure classifications of boom defence rating and surveyor recorder – all known as 'non-substantive' rates. Advancement through the specialism usually, but not always, went in step with substantive promotions, from Third through to First Class and ultimately, Instructor.

In the late 1940s during one of its spasmodic flirtations with new-fangled ideas, the Navy introduced psychology-based aptitude tests to aid its selection of young seamen for specialization. WRNS officers and ratings were trained to do this. I remember my own selection interview in RN barracks, conducted by an excitingly masterful petty officer Wren. Before testing, we went through the usual Navy charade of stating a preference. Surveyor recorder had appealed to me, as it was out of the ordinary and I had had considerable experience of chartwork during a spell as navigator's yeoman in my previous ship. However, I had recently heard from a former messmate who wrote from HMS *Harrier*, a radar and aircraft direction school perched on the Pembrokeshire cliffs near St Anne's Head, in such glowing terms that I revised my first choice to that of radar plot. On such slight and superficial considerations do the young make life-choices; I might have spent the next ten years getting a tan in open boats, charting tropical reefs in some South Seas archipelago – and, like most ex-naval recorders, found a well-paid job outside when the time came.

A brief written test and interview followed, wherein sheep were separated from goats, and eight out of ten of our batch were driven, bleating, to the gunnery school which was virtually no one's choice and consequently always had the most vacancies. I actually got what I asked for, and in due course received instructions to 'travel and report' to HMS *Harrier*. My oppo's testimonial, given that it was coloured to some extent by his having recently met his future wife (a stunningly attractive Wren) there, as did many RP ratings, was not much exaggerated. *Harrier* occupied a remote, windy eyrie a mile or so from the small fishing village of Dale, which comprised a cluster of cottages, a beach and the only public house for twelve miles. The school consisted of widely scattered groups of prefabricated single-storey buildings, giving it more the appearance of a wartime RAF airfield than a naval 'stone frigate' and the whole was surrounded by a high wire fence to comply with Customs regulations, duty-free privileges being enjoyed there as in most RN shore-establishments at that date.

The setting was not all that was untypical about HMS *Harrier*. The radar plot branch was a young one, free of hidebound tradition such as governed the gunnery schools. During the war the early radar sets in warships were installed and their operation supervised by 'boffins' – often civilians, or scientists masquerading as naval officers. The operators were selected from the more intelligent ratings, regardless of branch, and trained *in situ*. Many of these pioneer operators were sick-berth attendants. Jack insisted that they were selected because of their indifference to the rumoured effect on male gonads of high-frequency radar diffusions.

With the postwar development of radar, its strategic rather than purely tactical potential became apparent, and the Admiralty set up numerous plotting stations ashore. These were manned by Wrens, who could not then serve afloat; this resulted in there being many more Wrens than ratings in the branch. Combined with the fact that *Harrier* was also the school for meteorological recorders (all Wrens), this resulted in a girl-boy ratio of nearly three to one during my time there, which was incredibly nice for the boys. Remote as the establishment was, with a liberty-bus once a week to Haverfordwest and bicycles the only other mode of transport, off-duty amusements tended to be home-made. Here in *Harrier* was Jack's Fiddler's Green – turf underfoot, a wet canteen and two hundred well brought-up young women. (I was young for my age, and preferred nesting for gulls' eggs.) There was a thriving drama group, a Scottish dancing society known to the irreverent as the 'arse 'n' tartan club' and a weekly dance in the canteen, music by the West Cambrian Syncopators of Milford Haven.

Not that it was all lotus-eating in *Harrier*; the training course was demanding and many dogwatch hours were spent in study. Quite a large part of our working day was occupied in marching from place to place among the scattered buildings – accommodation site to instructional block to administration offices – and that in itself was pleasurable enough to one accustomed to the narrow steel confines of a warship. Walking the breezy cliff paths in the early summer sun, with springy turf and masses of wild flowers underfoot, I marvelled that two shore establishments such as His Majesty's Ships *Harrier* and *Ganges*, the notorious boys' training barracks still fresh in my 18-year-old memory, could exist in the same Navy.

Final examinations and passing-out came all too soon. I scored average marks and on my last evening in *Harrier*, sat on my bed sewing my RP3 badge – a red worsted spider's web with stylized sparks issuing from its four corners and single star above – onto the left sleeve of my jumper. I was alone in the hut; most of my classmates, celebrating in the wet canteen, had theirs sewn on for them.

Even after the rationalization and closures of redundant wartime training establishments referred to in the previous chapter, there were scores remaining, nearly all on or close to the south coast. They covered every aspect of naval expertise at every level from new entrant to commissioned warrant rank, in all branches of the service. Some provided joint training, like HMS *Phoenix*, the ABCD (Atomic, Biological and Chemical Defence) school commissioned at Tipnor, Portsmouth in 1948. Every rating, of whatever branch, was required to qualify at *Phoenix* in fire-fighting and damage control (the importance of which was learned the hard way during the war), in addition to learning about what little defence then existed against the new horrors of radioactive fallout and germ warfare. Damage control had previously been the responsibility of the shipwright, or 'chippie', who was later to be grandiosely designated 'hull engineer artificer' soon after the humble Stoker became an Engineering Mechanic. In the increasingly technical postwar Navy – and no doubt as an aid to recruitment – any rating who handled any tool, it seemed, was an engineer. (Except for the dab-toe seaman with his chipping-hammer, who would not have wished to be a superstructure surface-enhancing engineer.)

There were torpedo schools at HMS *Vernon*, Portsmouth, which also dealt with mining and all things explosive except shells, and *Defiance* at Devonport. An important postwar amalgamation was that of the torpedo and anti-submarine branches. Torpedoes had been around for a long time; Asdic (sonar) was, like radar, a wartime development. But the new A/S branch, mindful of its achievements against the Atlantic U-boats, was unwilling to accept what it saw as subordination to an old-established branch with only a tenuous association with its own function.[2] Ill-feeling between the two specialisms was exacerbated by the fact that torpedomen were eligible to transfer to the new electrical branch currently being set up, while anti-submarine operators were not, despite their being trained and experienced maintainers of their own equipment. For this and other reasons, *Vernon* was not a happy place to be at that time.

One of the other reasons was that in pursuance of the Admiralty's desire to return as soon as might be to peacetime (i.e. pre-war) standards of regulation and discipline, a 'new-broom' Commander-in-Chief, Adm. Sir Geoffrey Layton, had been appointed in 1946 to 'shake up Portsmouth Command'.[3] A newly-appointed executive officer, Cdr. George Blundell, found that at *Vernon*: '. . . the general efficiency was abysmal. The standard of dress, the discipline generally and morale was at a low ebb. Hundreds of ancient, passed over for promotion, torpedo officers swarmed everywhere offering helpful advice. Chief and petty officers, many long overdue for 'time expired', far outnumbered others in the ship's company. After the battering the place had received, it was all entirely predictable.'

A forceful, reforming new captain and Cdr. Blundell, between them, went through HMS *Vernon* like the proverbial dose of salts, knocking heads together, cutting out dead wood and generally improving morale. The two opposing elements were soon working well together in a new torpedo anti-submarine (TAS) branch and *Vernon*, which had been threatened with closure, was to survive for another fifty productive years.

The gunnery branch was still the biggest of the seaman branch specialisms, with the fabled Whale Island gunnery school in Portsmouth harbour, HMS *Excellent*, its Mecca and promised land. Presumably some seamen, a few, actually chose gunnery but most (unlike their officers) were forced into it. Legends of 'Whaley' abound: the vast parade square which was holy ground, the domain of parade chief gunnery instructors who wore whistles on chains around their necks which when peremptorily blown, followed by a scream of 'Still!', froze every sailor within five hundred yards in mid-motion, like a game of 'statues' or a Bad Fairy's spell. The god-like Parade Commander with his henchmen the dagger Gunners[4] always in attendance, stamping, bellowing, squealing; sending belted, gaitered, rifle-toting sailors pounding at the double across the gravel in all directions . . . pandemonium! Of course the Guards Depot could do as well, if not better – but it all seemed so unsailor-like. Whale Island was just a flesh-creeping legend among other branches with a higher average IQ, but most gunnery ratings took a perverse pride in having survived Whaley's rigours and emerged with a higher rate. (The regime may in fact not have been all that exhausting, to judge by the number of Portsmouth 'natives' among its alumni who claimed to have sneaked home in the dinner-hour to 'give the missus one with me boots an' gaiters on'.) The following reminiscence mentions the famous – perhaps fabulous – Whale Island parrot, which figures in many recollections:

HMS *Excellent* (Whale Island). Gun-fodder. Not many memories of this period. All shouting, doubling, crashing of boots and rifle-butts, Chief and PO GIs with whistles and swagger-sticks, officers with shiny black gaiters, whistles and swagger-sticks; all full of p*** and importance. Main memory is of an aviary on a hill above the parade ground with some parrots or parakeets, whatever. One used to hang from the overhead cage bars yelling, 'Help!' Another used to mimic the parade ground orders of loud-mouthed GIs. Sometimes on a Sunday divisions his voice would be heard calling the guard to attention.

Finish course, pass, sew badge on arm, seaman gunner Quarters 3rd Class. Now qualified to do a job that I had been doing for two years on *Mermaid.* Was it necessary? However, on completion back to RNB. Four weeks leading seaman course, early Easter leave and off to join *Modeste.*

(R. Grevett, Able Seaman, HMS *Excellent* 1956)

AB Grevett's hob-nailed ordeal was in fact necessary, as he could not qualify for advancement to leading hand until he had a non-substantive rating.

After *Montclare* I went on course to Whale Island where we were expected every fourth night to do a spell on sentry duty. Imagine dozens of sailors doing 'silly' jobs like: patrolling 100 yards of foreshore, the victualling block, pig farm, stores office and so on. Next day we had no make-and-mend, so sat in class yawning our heads off and not taking too much in. Later the night watch was changed to a killick and two riding around on bikes, with eight more sailors in the guardroom fully booted and spurred, lying on bunks unless called out.

After Whale Island I was sent 300 yards to join HMS *Cleopatra,* a 5,000-ton cruiser and part of the Reserve Fleet. We never moved from the jetty.

(C. Taylor, Able Seaman, HMS *Excellent* 1954)

There was life outside Whale Island:

Soon after . . . my endeavours to transfer for training as a radar mechanic were approved, and I was seconded to the ship's electrical branch to work with the radar/radio maintenance staff for the remainder of the commission, when on arrival back in UK I was promised a draft to HMS *Collingwood* to join a course for radar mechanic training.

Unfortunately, before we arrived back at Chatham the rate 'Radar Mechanic' became obsolete and the electrical branch proper had been formed with Radar Artificers and Radar Electrician's Mates taking their place. All training places were over-subscribed at *Collingwood* so I elected to train as an Electrician's Mate at the school in Chatham barracks, which was my only chance of technical training. And so began the second phase of my 24 years of naval service.

(G. Jay, Able Seaman, HMS *Phoebe* 1948)

Jay was one of those relatively well-educated seamen who had gained a school certificate before enlisting as a boy at age 15 and who, like Crew in Chapter 3 above, had the intelligence and aptitude to make a good technician but had to struggle hard to achieve his ambition, having joined at the wrong time and wrong level before such opportunities existed. Ex-yachtie Jay's subsequent career demonstrates how wasted he would have been in the seaman branch. After a period in the MoD as a quality assurance overseer covering contracts for naval equipment and armed with an Open University science degree obtained during five years' part-time study, he ended his career in the team up-dating and improving the 'Sea Dart' missile system and associated radar for the New Navy. Long before that, however, still in the old Navy:

> After doing my provisional exams for leading hand I was then drafted to HMS *Collingwood*, the RN electrical school near Fareham in Hampshire, a huge establishment with nearly 3,000 people accommodated at any one time and the biggest parade ground in the UK, to do my LEM's course.
>
> Despite the fact that we were in wooden huts, one class to a hut, it was my first experience of relative comfort in the service. The huts were warm and spacious with proper lockers and good bathing facilities with plenty of hot water, drying rooms for our dhobeying and generally firm but not oppressive discipline from senior rates. The sports and recreational facilities were excellent and we had really top names of the time to entertain us at *Collingwood* theatre. The food however was still atrocious and the excellent NAAFI canteen, which did simple cooked meals, was always full in the evening.
>
> The course was very demanding. It covered a lot of ground in depth and standards of teaching and examinations were high.
>
> (G. Jay, Electrical Mechanic, HMS *Collingwood* 1952)

Here, a few miles from Whale Island but seemingly a world away, was a modern training establishment with a modern-minded staff teaching the new skills required in an atomic-age Navy, with only the victualling staff reassuringly flying the flag for the old Navy. Extraordinary that *Collingwood*'s galley and its cooks could not provide palatable food while the NAAFI manager, who also had to make a profit, could! Naval cooks were trained too, but badly, if the results were anything to go by. HMS *Ceres*, the vast Supply and Secretariat School at Wetherby in Yorkshire, was responsible for training miscellaneous ratings, including cooks. But there was no Jago expertise to spare at *Ceres* for seaman cooks;

recruits were instructed by chief and warrant cooks themselves brought up in the naval 'slushy' tradition, who made sure to pass on their own bad habits intact. There was simply no need for this, given that officers' cooks were trained at the same establishment to the very high standards demanded by the wardroom; some of the skill available might surely have been expended on making Jack's fare a little more appetizing. But the lowly status of the cook branch in the Supply and Secretariat hierarchy and the whole philosophy of naval victualling made such a thing impossible, until much needed and long-overdue reforms were instituted in the late 1950s. Writers were much more highly regarded, and better-trained, as a Writer's competence, or want of it, affected his officers in a way which the quality of a messdeck dinner did not.

We had a mass of stuff to learn between July and November that would enable us – and it proved so in my case before long – to go to a ship and take over an empty space, equip it with all that was needed to become a Ship's Office and for us to act, alone if necessary, as a Captain's secretary and to deal with all the incoming, circulation, filing and outgoing of mail to and from the ship to anywhere. To establish a comprehensive system of filing and documentation of the ship's company's personal data as well as that of, and pertaining to, the ship. To keep all *King's/Queen's Regulations & Admiralty Instructions*, Admiralty Fleet Orders etc. up to date, and to have to hand and attend with all the documents and information the Captain or other officers might need at 'Captain's Table' which handled all requests and punishments. It was even necessary to know by heart the procedures for Admiral's office or courts martial which might fall to our lot in the future. All of this of course required detailed knowledge of all the multitude of forms used within the Navy – quite a task in itself – also the standard punishment scales laid down for specific breaches of 'good order and naval discipline' – how long one got for what!

I did pretty well, coming out with results, in all sections, in the higher 70s, which gave me 'Captain's office work' as my grading and thus the lower-graded Pay Office, Drafting and Ship's Office work as a matter of course. I was quite satisfied and hoping for my first draft to be aboard ship, preferably a destroyer (not too big and not too small!) without too much 'bull' but large enough to warrant a Writer on the complement (in smaller ships than that the Captain's office 'Writer' was often a reasonably well-educated seaman).

(M. Bree, Probationary Writer, HMS *Ceres* 1947)

Alas for newly-fledged Writer Bree, who was soon to be disabused of the notion that training-school markings cut any ice in the Drafting Office! His first job was about as far from captain's office in a destroyer as a Writer could get; namely, the Pay Office in RN Barracks. There was no malice in this; the Drafting Office was not run by human emotion, but by sheer blind chance.

The training commitment was sometimes uneven. It was perfectly possible – indeed it was common – for a postwar rating to spend half his service on training courses of one sort or another, while some were denied what they considered essential training:

> Looking back I'm surprised at the lack of training, as I've said before you were expected to pick it up on the job. Yet you had periods between ships when all you were doing was menial tasks like cleaning machinery spaces on ships that were being scrapped, painting coal white, etc. You looked forward to being in the barracks but after some time you were glad to be out of it. I'm sure some of this idle time could have been used for training. They used to offer engine-room ratings a diesel course but that was almost certainly a way to get you into submarines. You had to volunteer for subs but during this course pressure was brought to bear for you to do so. We kept well away from it.
>
> (B. Whitworth, Stoker Mechanic, HMS *Drake* 1952)

SM Whitworth was, of course, experiencing the universal 'make-work' referred to in Chapter 3 when he was cleaning machinery soon to be attacked with cutting equipment, and white-washing coal – all sailors did their share of that. But he does appear justified in feeling deprived of necessary training in the duties he was expected to perform, sight unseen, on joining a new ship:

> Drafts came out of the blue, no warning at all. In the barracks you'd be lined up and handed a draft chit and off you went. No training, totally unprepared. I was drafted to *Ark Royal* to commission her after being built in Camell Laird of Birkenhead. Being an engine-room rating I fully expected to be in the engine-room. I was completely unprepared to find myself on the flight-deck, fuelling planes. When you joined you had very basic training and then, it appeared, you had to pick it up on the job. *Euryalus* was steam turbine-driven, *Enard Bay* had triple-expansion engines, *Ark Royal* – I didn't even see the engine-room. No wonder we needed months to work-up the *Ark Royal*.

A stoker in the Royal Navy was a lowly being and was certainly made to feel it. Considering the acknowledged excellence of the Navy's school for artificers at HMS *Caledonia* and the courses for engineer officers at the Naval Engineering College, Manadon, the engine-room branch seemed to have little time and effort left for its junior members, apart from making them bitterly regret joining at *Imperieuse* and calling them Engineering Mechanics to improve recruitment.

During the war and after, instructor officers played an increasing role in nearly all areas of training. They were schoolmasters in uniform, university graduates for the most part in an era when a naval officer with a degree was as rare as one with an inferiority complex, which is to say rare but not unknown. They wore distinguishing pale-blue cloth between their rank stripes and were rather looked-down upon by 'real' naval officers of the executive branch. A very few instructor officers went to sea in aircraft-carriers as meteorological officers, or in other big ships as tutors to midshipmen in mathematics and navigation. The great majority served ashore in a variety of teaching capacities, from classroom coaching of ratings who needed the educational certificates for advancement, to Senior Instructors overseeing courses for officers and senior rates in the new, highly technical branches. They were experts, of course, in their own field of educational theory and course-structure; an expertise much-needed in the Navy of that date. Many of them were Welsh.

There were two such on the staff at HMS *Harrier*, both instructor lieutenants and both, like 42.68 per cent of Welshmen, called Jones. To distinguish them, one was known as 'Moto Jones' because of his pronunciation of 'motor', as in 'electric moto'; the younger was 'Tobacco Jones' because the first lieutenant had given him responsibility for the ratings' monthly soap and tobacco issue. Both instructed the courses in radar theory. 'Moto' was very Welsh in appearance, speech and mannerism. He was fortyish, short, stocky, dark and balding. He had been a schoolmaster in his native Rhondda and was one of the pioneers of the multiple-choice examination-paper. As an experiment he gave a specimen paper full of arcane radar-theory questions to a group of new arrivals awaiting training, to confirm his theory that answers selected randomly by ratings with no knowledge of the subject would score between 28 and 31 per cent. He may have put this empirical information gained to some schoolmasterly use.

Largely at the instigation of the 'schoolies', instructional technique was much improved, with instructors of all branches being brought together for short courses in practice lecturing, which also now featured in the petty officers' leadership course at HMS *Royal Arthur*,

Corsham. A huge programme of 'training the trainers' was introduced in the mid-1950s as new weapons and equipment were brought into service. Even the gunnery branch was to experience the wind of change, eventually; losing its 'gas and gaiters' attitude as it had to think electronic.

CHAPTER NINE

'Make the Navy Your Korea'

Between 1946 and 1960 numerous actions, incidents and small wars occurred during which sailors were killed or injured, from the Corfu Channel incident in October 1946, to Suez, via the Korean war. Of course, there was nothing during those peacetime years to remotely compare with the two World Wars or the long drawn-out attrition of the Battle of the Atlantic with its fearful toll of naval and merchant seamen alike. But if you got killed in a small war rather than in a major one, you were just as dead.

First, in the aftermath of the Second World War:

Unlike the Army and RAF, peacetime took a lot longer to assimilate in the Navy, largely because our boundaries were so far-flung, and although both Enemies had surrendered, what they'd left behind hadn't, namely the mines, the wrecks, the littered harbours, the personnel who had to be sorted and distributed back to where they belonged. There were no long-distance jet planes then to fly them home and replace war-weary troops with fresh faces.

The Navy had it to sort out, *on its own*! Did you know the last escorted convoy to sail from the UK was in February 1946? Why? Well, the Bay of Biscay and the Med were still full of floating mines and other war-debris. So warships had to go ahead of the merchantmen to allay any anxiety to ships' passengers. A remarkable sight to see a whole convoy fully lit-up, cruising along at a stately 15 knots!

Between 1945 and 1960, the majority of HM ships' configuration altered little, though there were many ambitious plans afoot regarding modernisation and altogether new design, with the prospect of more weaponry in view. That came later.

(F. Woods, Stoker, HMS *Superb* 1946)

With VJ Day still a recent memory, cold war confrontation was already beginning, and with most of the world, apart from a few uneasily 'non-aligned' nations firmly in opposing camps, any small conflagration was all too likely to cause a dangerous increase in the temperature. The first of these was lit in May 1946 and involved Albania, a poverty-stricken, backward Balkan state with a recently-elected communist government which followed the Soviet line and was rabidly anti-West. British warships regularly steamed the narrow channel between the island of Corfu and the Greek mainland while on passage between the Adriatic and the Mediterranean in the course of mine-clearance in those two seas, for which Britain had been given responsibility by the newly-formed International Mine Clearance Board. Albania had applied for representation on this body, but had been refused because she had no navy and no money to contribute towards the cost; also, Britain together with the USA had recently vetoed her membership of the United Nations and consequently anti-British feeling ran high.

On 14 May two British cruisers, *Superb* and *Orion*, were negotiating the channel when they were fired upon by an Albanian coastal battery. No hits were scored and the warships did not return the fire. There followed, however, a strong protest by the British government to Albania, who claimed unconvincingly that the cruisers had been mistaken for Greek minesweepers, which the Albanians suspected of piracy! After the diplomatic kerfuffle had subsided, with Albania being warned that if British ships were again fired on in what were recognized as international waters they would return fire, the Mediterranean Fleet's autumn cruise provided a suitable opportunity to test President Hoxha's good faith, or lack of it. A detached component of the fleet paying a courtesy visit to Corfu had orders on departure to proceed northabout round the island and, in what was essentially a coat-trailing exercise, to steam south through the channel en route to Argostoli for the fleet regatta. The ships had orders to go through with guns trained fore and aft, but to open fire if fired upon.

During the afternoon of 22 October, the cruiser *Mauritius* flying the flag of Rear-Adm. Kinehan, flag officer 15th Cruiser Squadron, entered the Corfu Channel with the destroyer *Saumarez* close astern. Astern of them were the cruiser *Leander* and another destroyer, *Volage*.

At some point there occurred a violent explosion accompanied by a sheet of flame just forward of *Saumarez*'s bridge and a fire was soon raging aboard. Although the ships were proceeding carefully down the middle of the charted swept channel, it was clear that *Saumarez* had struck a mine. With some difficulty she was taken in tow by *Volage* and the two destroyers headed slowly toward open waters. Having covered only a short distance, *Volage* also struck a mine which blew her bows off but, thanks to outstanding damage control by her crew, did not sink. In due course, all four ships returned safely to harbour, but the casualty toll in the two mined ships was forty officers and ratings killed, with another forty-three injured.

Subsequently, the Mediterranean Fleet's minesweepers carried out an intensive sweep for mines in the Corfu Channel, with a neutral observer present. Twenty-two mines were swept up, which on examination proved to be of German origin, and recently-laid. It was clear that these mines had been deliberately sown in a previously-swept channel. Albania denied responsibility but the International Court at The Hague eventually found against them and the UK was awarded compensation which Albania has never paid. Her guilt, however, is beyond question:

It was after one of the Med Fleet's 'exercises' and show of force in the Adriatic, steaming through the Corfu Channel on the way to the Greek islands for R&R that two of our destroyers, *Volage* and *Saumarez* both hit mines in rapid succession with the result that they both lost their bows; up to the bridge in the case of *Saumarez* and up to 'B' turret on *Volage*, with large loss of life. It was 'Action Stations' again naturally enough, and all the cruisers were ready to open fire on the Albanian shore batteries which were showing signs of frantic activity. In the event there was no exchange of fire, and the two boats were towed back to Malta where *Saumarez* was scapped and *Volage* had a new bow fitted.

The channel was swept immediately and the mines were found to be brand new, they had only been in the water for a very short time.

(C. Jay, Able Seaman, HMS *Phoebe* 1946)

This whole incident and its outcome illustrates how the balance of power in the world had shifted since before the war and how diminished Great Britain's power and authority had become since then. An affront such as this, an act of war by a minor country such as Albania, would have brought swift and crushing retribution, and prompt reparation. Now, one had to consider the likely reaction of the Soviet Union to an attack on one of its vassal states and even if the UK had been inclined to retaliate no doubt the United States, new leader of the free world, would have urged restraint, as she was later to do in the case of Suez. Poor Britain, getting the worst of all worlds as usual! For though her power, wealth and prestige had become one (as her imperial poet predicted), with Nineveh and Tyre, the leftover burdens and obligations of Empire had still to be attended to.

Not far away, in the eastern Mediterranean, a confrontation of a different kind was building up. Since 1922 when the League of Nations had laid upon Britain the task of administrating Palestine, the level of Jewish immigration had been controlled by the British in order to maintain a balance of population between Jew and Arab, as the Mandate required. With the end of the war there were hundreds of thousands of Jewish 'displaced persons', mostly from eastern European states and most survivors of German concentration camps who had had more than enough of persecution and longed to settle in Israel, the promised land. Illegal immigration, which had always taken place, now increased sharply, threatening the fragile sufferance of the two races, one for the other. The illegals were embarked in a motley collection of barely seaworthy ships of all nationalities, usually in southern European ports, which would then sail, laden to the gunwhales with men, women and children in the most insanitary conditions, to beach themselves on any accessible part of the Palestinian coastline. The conditions on board these rotting rust-buckets, not insured at Lloyds or anywhere else, became after a few days indescribably filthy. It was said that 'the stench could be smelt for miles, which thus often gave early warning of the proximity of an illegal immigrant ship'.[1]

The situation ashore soon reached crisis proportions, with terrorists from both sides active; and the Palestine police, aided by the Army, could barely contain it. The Navy was called in, with destroyers of the Mediterranean Fleet based on the port of Haifa, each one allocated a twenty-mile stretch of coast to patrol, charged with the unpopular task of intercepting, boarding, and turning back immigrant ships. In many cases the desperate immigrants, within sight of the longed-for haven, resisted fiercely, and by any underhand means. The scratch boarding parties were destroyer sailors and not paratroopers or Royal Marines; famously good with children when entertaining them and their civilian parents at shipboard parties and Navy Days, they were shocked by the reception they received. They were met with a variety of weapons from scalding steam hoses to iron bars, axes and knives. In violent pitched battles both sailors and immigrants were often injured and sometimes killed. Many ratings gained hurt-certificates as souvenirs of their Palestine service; I saw one endorsed, in the section for medical officer's remarks: 'Severe abdominal contusions caused by illegal immigrants jumping on his stomach'.

Belatedly, the destroyer crews were given training by Royal Marine commandos in self-defence and boarding techniques; they were also issued with shields, steel helmets, coshes and revolvers. They now knew what a desperately difficult mission it was to board against fierce resistance a ship whose every square foot of deck-space was crammed with humanity; where sailors gaining a toe-hold were sometimes hoisted aloft, passed from hand to hand above the massed bodies and dumped into the sea on the far side. Sometimes it was a case of kill or be killed, as related by a young Ordinary Seaman:[2]

I don't know exactly which boarding I went over with but it was the one after Lt. Soames got over. I jumped on to a sloping raft 15–25 feet above the funnel starboard side. The raft was on skids and as soon as I was on it so were six thugs from inboard. They had been hiding behind the raft and so escaped notice. One hopped right past me to the starboard side or lower end of the raft, which was a silly thing to do as I booted him over the side. After I had cleared the raft I became the target for pretty much everything, bar the mess kettle. I tried to get inboard three times but there was too much opposition. I was forced to draw my revolver and fired eleven warning rounds. One of the last shots, however, I used to stop a lad of seventeen or eighteen from collecting my scalp with a meat axe. He got it in the stomach. I am sorry about that, but it was him or me. When they slipped the raft I must have passed out, although I remember jumping clear of the raft in mid-air. The *Cardigan Bay* (which had been stationed as long stop) picked me up at 0430.

This young rating did not exaggerate his ordeal; when *Cardigan Bay*'s boat recovered him from the raft, his face was a bloody pulp with both eyes closed up and he had two bad gashes on his head as evidence of the meat axe.

The Haifa patrol lasted for nearly two years, until the British Mandate was terminated on 14 May 1948. For Jack, it was arguably the most hazardous duty he was ever called upon to perform in the postwar period, not excluding various 'hot' wars, and certainly the most unpleasant. Many sailors bore the scars of their experiences, physical and mental, for years to come.

Another of the postwar world's trouble-spots in which the Royal Navy found itself caught up was China. The Chinese had, of course, been at war continously, first against the Japanese and then with each other, since 1937. The communist Chinese under Mao Tse-tung, armed with captured Japanese weaponry, were steadily pushing the Nationalist forces southward, and by April had driven them across the Yangtse river. Previously, when Chiang Kai-shek was still in power, it had been agreed with the Nationalists that the UK, together with other foreign powers who still had commercial interests, and citizens, in China should maintain their ambassadors and consular officials there. Permission was also obtained to station a British warship at Nanking (see page 88) for the protection and, if necessary, the evacuation of British nationals. In April 1949 this guardship was the destroyer HMS *Consort*, which was overdue for relief, with supplies running low. The frigate *Amethyst*, Lt. Cdr. Bernard Skinner in command, was detailed for this relief.

The situation along the Yangtse was tense, with the opposing forces facing each other from the opposite banks. The UK authorities had attempted to secure a guarantee of safe passage for *Amethyst*, without success, but because of *Consort's* situation she was ordered to proceed. On 19 April she sailed from Shanghai, flying two oversize White Ensigns and with large Union flags painted on both sides of her hull. Despite this clear identification, early next morning, when still some sixty miles from Nanking, communist batteries on the north bank opened fire at short range, scoring hits and causing severe damage and casualties, among them the captain and *Amethyst's* doctor, both of whom died from their injuries. A shell struck the low power room, putting the ship's steering, gyro-compass and fire control system out of action, and the frigate ran aground on a sandbank, Her badly-wounded first lieutenant ordered some of the crew to land, together with those wounded who were able to do so, and this they did, still under fire from communist machine-guns. *Amethyst's* 'flash' signal to base at Shanghai that she was being fired on stimulated frantic activity there. First, *Consort* was ordered to proceed with all despatch to *Amethyst's* aid. She arrived on the scene in a couple of hours to be promptly fired upon by the communist batteries, and during a gallant but unsuccessful attempt to take the frigate in tow, sustained damage which compelled her to abandon the attempt and escape down river. On the way, she encountered the cruiser HMS *London* flying the flag of Vice Adm. Madden, second-in-command Far East Fleet, accompanied by *Black Swan* frigate, heading at full speed up river, and was ordered to continue to Shanghai. Before this new force could reach the stranded frigate, it too came under heavy and accurate shelling. Fire was returned, but after a short, sharp duel in which both ships took damage and casualties, Vice Adm. Madden broke off the action to avoid further loss of life, and returned to Shanghai.

There now followed several weeks of stalemate, during which an RAF Sunderland aircraft bravely essayed a landing alongside *Amethyst* and, under fire, managed to transfer an RAF doctor with medical supplies and a few key personnel before successfully taking off again and returning to Hong Kong.[3] The assistant naval attaché at Nanking, Lt. Cdr. J.S. Kerans, had been ordered to proceed overland from there to take command. *Amethyst*, now refloated and at anchor, was ordered to remain where she was pending diplomatic attempts to secure her safe passage. It was Lt. Cdr. Keran's thankless task to attend endless meetings with communist officials to negotiate this; fruitlessly, because he refused, with the full backing of the Commander-in-Chief, Adm. Sir Patrick Brind, to concede that *Amethyst* was guilty of infringing Chinese sovereignty and should accept blame for the incident. This dragged on for three months.

Supplies on *Amethyst* were running out and fuel getting low when Kerans determined on an escape attempt. It would obviously be extremely hazardous and Kerans first consulted his crew, who were unanimously in favour.

After nightfall on 30 July, *Amethyst* stealthily slipped her greased and muffled cable and glided off down river. What happened next is best described by OS Gordon 'Shiner' Wright:[4]

We slipped anchor just after ten in the evening. We had to do a full turn. That was the most frightening part of all – we could easily have been blown out of the water by their 75 mm and 105 mm guns. I was in the wheelhouse all the way down: I'll never forget that turn. We didn't create very big waves, in fact we turned very slowly, very skilful navigation work. My divisional officer was Sub-Lieutenant Hett, who was only twenty or twenty-one. He was working with charts that were ripped and covered with blood, and he had no charts of the river at all, they were all lost. He really should have got more recognition because he got us through even though he wasn't a navigation officer.

So there we were, going down the river in the dark. We passed a local boat which had all its lights on. The communists started firing at this boat. They must have been quite stupid – if we were going to escape we would never put lights on a ship. The skipper said, 'Right, we'll go on now. Let them take it.' You could hear the shells come over the ship. Franks said to me, 'Now, Shiner, if anything happens to me you get on this wheel.' I said to him, 'It's being so bloody cheerful that keeps you going.'

When we were halfway down, just before we got to Kiang Yin, there was a boom right across the river. I heard Cdr. Kerans say to Hett, 'There's a boom here, we've got to more or less guess which side to take, and hope for the best.' I think they decided to go on the starboard side. In the wheelhouse we were lying on the deck so that if anything happened we'd already be on the deck. Luckily they chose the right side.

It was still dark, it didn't start getting light till half-past five in the morning. I then heard Kerans say that if we got to Woosung Fort it would be the most critical point of the breakout, because they had 9-inch guns which could blow us out of the water if they caught us in their searchlights. Then we heard him say, 'Woosung in sight.' I had my fingers crossed. We got past them, they must have been asleep or something, or the communications were bad. Their big guns did not fire. Kerans then came over the intercom: 'I want every man to give everything for the last leg.'

While we were passing Woosung, HMS *Concord* was there. They had been told that if Woosung ever started firing at us they were to blast at its guns. There was cheering, of course, when it came by. I don't know how we did it, I never thought for one minute we were going to make it, it was beyond my wildest dreams. I said to Franks, 'Never thought we were going to make it,' and the tears were pouring down my face. I couldn't stop shaking. Open sea at last, fresh air. I can't really put into words how I felt. Relief, relief to think we were going to have some fresh food, plenty to eat. When we got alongside the boys in *Consort* they said, with great smiles on their faces, 'Right, what do you want to eat? We'll bring some stuff over.' The sirens were going, the hooters were going.

Believe it or not, if it had taken half-an-hour longer we would have run out of fuel. We just had enough. But we had lost 23 out of a ship's company of 183.

Lt. Cdr. Kerans sent out one final message: 'HAVE REJOINED THE FLEET. AM SOUTH OF WOOSUNG. NO DAMAGE OR CASUALTIES. GOD SAVE THE KING.'

This famous signal, so pride-stirring to British hearts at a time when patriotism seemed to have little to feed upon, was the headline in all the next day's newspapers, at home and abroad. Lt. Cdr. Kerans was decorated and promoted full commander. Quitting while ahead, he resigned soon after in order to stand for Parliament, where for several years he was an active and useful backbencher with an interest in naval matters.

The Naval Prayer asks for deliverance from 'the dangers of the sea and the violence of the enemy'. The latter is sporadic; the former ever-present in a hazardous environment, where disaster strikes when least expected, as illustrated by the *Illustrious* liberty-boat calamity (Chapter 5) and by the following:

As far as I can recall we had lost only one man killed. We were routinely entering harbour in the Clyde during work-up. So routinely that the commander was holding a defaulters' parade at the time. We had almost reached our anchorage and the starboard motor boat was turned out on the davits. The screws were still turning. Suddenly the after fall parted from the bottom of the motor boat and its stern fell, leaving the bow hanging from the davit head. The sternsheetsman, Able Seaman Wing, was thrown into the water. I was by then an ST (Seaman Torpedoman) and standing by the starboard torpedo tubes. I looked over the side. AB Wing was in the water sliding towards the

HMS *London*

stern unable to swim, hampered by his oilskin. The ship's screws
were still turning. I saw him sucked down. He was never seen again.
Able Seaman Wing was a popular lad, just 19 years old with thick
black hair and of Chinese descent. A sad story.

(J. Crew, Able Seaman, HMS *Arethusa* 1946)

A particularly dangerous trade during war and peace is that of the
submarine branch. The war at sea took its toll of British submarines as it
did of the surface fleet, but peacetime loss of surface ships through
accident is rare indeed. Submarine sinkings, on the other hand, were all
too common in the inter-war years when Admiralty indecision about the
future role and purpose of submarines manifested itself in a succession of
giant, clumsy submersibles carrying battleship-size guns, even aircraft,
with untried technology which, as in the case of the notorious 'K' class,
all too often made them steel coffins for their unfortunate crews.

The last peacetime loss of a British submarine had been that of the
Thetis on 1 June 1939, which sank in Liverpool Bay during acceptance
trials with the loss of 99 lives, only two of those on board escaping. The
dead included civilian dockyard workers.[5] Then, in the early 1950s, two
disasters occurred within little more than a year of each other. Both were
as the result of collision with a surface vessel.

On the dark evening of 12 January 1950 HMS/M *Truculent* was
proceeding, surfaced, up the Thames Estuary from the Nore submarine
exercise area bound for Sheerness, when she collided with a Swedish
motor vessel. She was struck on the starboard bow, badly holed and

quickly sank. Her captain and four others of the crew who were on the bridge were thrown clear and soon picked up by a Dutch coaster. Meanwhile on the seabed the stricken submarine, her forward compartments flooded, had settled more or less upright. Most of her crew eventually made their escape from the aft spaces, using DSEA (Davis Submarine Escape Apparatus); unfortunately, because news of the sinking took over an hour to reach the authorities, there were no rescue vessels at the scene and most of the escapees were swept seaward on the strong Thames tide and drowned. One of those who did survive gives his terse account:

> I remember the *Bleasdale* going out to the Sub-Smash, but I was picked up by a Dutch liner about an hour after the collision. The one that hit us sailed on. I came up out of the conning tower and had a fifty feet swim to the surface, a freezing cold night, I still can't understand how we survived that, but we were all suffering from hypothermia when we were hauled inboard. Then taken up river and dropped off at Gravesend. (F. Henley, Leading Seaman, HMS/M *Truculent* 1950)

And from a bystander:

> But my main memory of Sheerness was the day the submarine *Truculent* sank in the Thames Estuary, close to the Isle of Sheppey, after colliding with a merchant ship. She went down in quite shallow water but most of her crew were lost. I remember standing on Cornwallis jetty watching her being towed into Sheerness dockyard after she was raised. Her conning tower and adjacent hull badly damaged. (G. Jay, Electrician's Mate, HMS *Duncansby Head* 1950)

The *Truculent* escapees were doubly unfortunate in that a recently-developed 'immersion suit' which would have helped them stay afloat and insulated them against hypothermia, had not yet been issued. The suits were available fifteen months later on board HMS/M *Affray*, but the unlucky crew and passengers were never to have the opportunity of testing them. *Affray*, a new submarine, was one of the large 'A' class boats built late in the war for service in the Pacific theatre, and when she left Portsmouth for a patrol exercise on 16 April 1951 she carried, in addition to her crew of fifty officers and ratings, a further twenty young officers under training plus four Royal Marines. Her orders were to proceed submerged down-channel to Falmouth, a passage which would take three days, part of it at periscope-depth employing her snort, or 'schnorkel' tube, copied from the German U-boats. Each morning she was to come to snorting depth and report her position by wireless.

When on the morning of the 17th she failed to do so, the routine 'Submiss' signal went out to alert rescue services, and after the elapse of two hours with nothing heard of or from the boat, 'Subsmash', which sent search aircraft, helicopters and surface vessels including the salvage ship *Reclaim* to her estimated position. Destroyers and frigates combed the area with their Asdic but there were so many sunken wartime wrecks in that part of the English Channel that they had an impossible task. Divers went down repeatedly on likely-looking contacts but none was *Affray*.

By 19 April, the day on which the missing submarine was to have arrived at Falmouth, it was accepted that all on board must have perished. The full-scale search was therefore stood down, but *Reclaim* continued with it, newly equipped with a vital aid – an improvised, rather Heath Robinson-ish underwater television camera hastily put together by clever members of the RN Scientific Service, which could be operated by remote control from *Reclaim*'s plotting-room. Now, when an underwater object was located by Asdic, the camera could be deployed to instantly identify it.

Two months after she disappeared, *Affray* was found. She was lying, upright, 300 feet down a few miles north-west of the island of Alderney, several miles off her planned course. Her snort-tube was in the raised position and was damaged in a way which indicated she had been in collision with a surface ship whilst snorting; also, there were no signs of an escape attempt having been made and her position-indicator buoys had not been released, which postulated a mercifully quick death for those within. One of the trainee officers on board was Sub-Lt. Frew, who was among the few survivors of the recent *Truculent* sinking. Given that *Truculent* and *Affray* were the only two British submarines to be lost since the war's end, this young man suffered the most extraordinary misfortune; to be spared once only to perish, mere months later, in a second, as if the dark sea were determined to have him.

As this tragedy in the English Channel unfolded, on the other side of the world a war was at its height. Korea had been a vassal state of the Japanese empire since 1910. However, since the latter's defeat in the Second World War, it had been effectively divided into two separate nations along the 38th Parallel. This was brought about by the Potsdam conference of 1945, at which it was agreed that Soviet Russia, which had recently and belatedly declared war on Japan, should receive the surrender of Japanese forces north of the parallel, and the USA those south of it. By 1948 North Korea had become a full-blown communist state with a large army equipped and trained by the Russians. To balance this, the United Nations established the democratic Republic of South Korea and the stage was set for confrontation.

This duly occurred on 25 June 1950 when North Korean troops attacked across the border, complete with tanks and jet fighters. They quickly overran the all but defenceless South, including the capital, Seoul, and had soon forced the defenders into little more than an enclave around the port of Pusan on the southern tip of the peninsula. At a hurriedly-called meeting of the United Nations Security Council, North Korea was ordered to withdraw immediately behind the 38th Parallel and, this demand being ignored, the UN's land, sea and air forces, led by the Americans, were quickly mobilized. During the next fifteen months the land-battle surged first one way, then the other, with the newly-emergent Chinese lending their weight whenever the North appeared to be facing defeat – but the land-battle has no place here, except insofar as it influenced naval operations.

British Army units would take time to be deployed but the Navy, in the shape of the Far East Fleet – still a considerable force in 1950 – was already to hand. Within a week of the UN resolution, the light fleet carrier *Triumph*; the cruisers *Belfast* and *Jamaica*, together with destroyers *Consort* and *Cossack* and the frigates *Alacrity*, *Hart* and *Black Swan*, plus auxiliaries, had placed themselves under the orders of the admiral commanding US Seventh Fleet. The navies of the Commonwealth and other NATO countries also provided warships. The North Koreans possessing only light naval forces, the Navy's role throughout the hostilities was confined to blockade, shore-bombardment and air strikes, with a Royal Marine commando doing useful work in spoiling raids on the enemy coast. The Fleet Air Arm had the closest continuous involvement at the 'sharp end' with their propeller-driven Fireflies and Sea Furies carrying out over 20,000 sorties before the truce was signed, losing 33 aircrew in the process. They mixed it with Russian MIG jet fighters, and actually shot one down. A Soviet-built bomber was accounted for by naval gunfire:

> Our sister ship, the *Jamaica*, had the distinction of shooting down one of the only two YAK planes which put in an appearance. *Jamaica* suffered minor damage and one serious casualty during the engagement. Able Seaman Godsall, the casualty, later succumbed to his wounds and he was buried at sea from *Kenya*'s quarterdeck on the 25 September. (D. Banks, Leading Stoker Mechanic, HMS *Kenya* 1950)

The cruiser *Kenya* was ordered up from Hong Kong to supplement the detached force early in September. One of her telegraphists recalls the first days on station:

Sailing from Hong Kong to the war zone, we were issued with BR827A Ship Safety booklet dated June 1943 and F/PW/80, a small buff card bearing your name and number 'If you are captured etc., etc.' The receipt of these documents signalled that this event was going to be somewhat different from the mundane Yangtse patrols. I did not keep a diary as we were ordered not to – my recollections therefore are based on a résumé prepared by our Number One (First Lieutenant) my few photos and of course, memory.

Our first sea days in Korean waters were as escort/tender to the carriers *Triumph* and *Theseus* and, much later, *Ocean*. These patrols were of nine to ten days at a time and because we operated so far out to sea, apart from Asdic and radar activity, we observed the unfortunate Seafire pilots who, on returning from sorties over Korea, had some horrendous deck-landings – in fact *Triumph* lost so many Seafires that she returned to the UK – *Theseus* was marginally 'luckier' but deck-landing fatalities were quite numerous. What sticks in my mind more than anything about those fatalities, is not only the poor sods who bought it, but the apparently uncaring attitude of the RN to the dependants. Why do I say that? In the W/T office we monitored the same ship-to-shore frequency as the carriers and within hours, sometimes less, of a fatal crash, a signal in plain language would be sent to base *cancelling* all pay and allowances to dependants! Cost-saving on defence budgets even then!

Although when working with the carriers we were at action stations, it was not quite real. Our very first 'Action Stations!' occurred when we were on patrol at night, well away from the coast and the danger of floating mines. The alarm sounded and we all closed up to our action stations, mine in the W/T office. We were able to follow events due to the reports from Radar being relayed over the loudspeaker system to the bridge – target bearings and speed were being called out at almost second intervals. The speed of the target seemed to increase with every report, and the target vessel did not respond to identification challenge. As we closed to what seemed chillingly-close range the captain ordered starshell to be fired. The target turned out to be a Chinese motorised junk, the 'Anhai'! A bit of an anticlimax – but we did make the newspapers, albeit described as American.'[6]

(C. Harrold, Ordinary Telegraphist, HMS *Charity* 1950)

Apart from air strikes, the most frequent operation undertaken by the allied warships in support of the Army was bombardment of enemy positions. In mid-September an amphibious landing was planned by the US Tenth Corps at Inchon on the west coast, with the objective of recapturing Seoul, cutting enemy communications and relieving pressure on the southern enclave. In preparation for a landing, the cruisers *Kenya*, *Jamaica* and *Ceylon* with an escorting screen of destroyers, and the carrier *Triumph* to provide air-spotting of shot, carried out a bombardment of the defences. Leading Stoker Mechanic D. Bank's account follows:

At 1300 we opened fire on gun positions on the mole at Inchon at about seven and a half miles range, and for the next half hour we fired at targets, mostly gun emplacements, in the dock area while the destroyers inshore of us kept up an almost continuous barrage from their 5-inch. Shore batteries were replying but so far without effect . . . the next news was that *Gurke* and *Collett* had been hit, so 'without effect' no longer applied. A few minutes before 1400 we were in a position to bring all three turrets to bear and managed to loose off two 9-gun salvoes before the order to cease fire came from the flagship – a second air strike was due to start. The destroyers now retired at high speed while still under fire from the shore batteries, of which there seemed to be plenty, and we learned that yet a third, *Swenson*, had been hit.

Attention was then turned to Wolmi-do, a wooded island off Inchon, a former pleasure-park now holding the batteries which had engaged the destroyers. In the meantime the latter had managed to get out of range to the seaward of us and while some were seen transferring their casualties to *Toledo* the rest were busy dealing with mines which were now visible all around . . . The destroyers bagged their first mine just before midday and round about that time *Toledo* joined with us in taking a crack at the two Wolmi-do batteries that were still engaging us. A minute or so after midday we stopped the left hand one and shortly afterwards our ammunition allowance for this particular job was expended.

This was not another case of the mangy old British lion having to make economies, but conservation of ammunition for other jobs in hand, until the ships could be replenished from their supply train.

For our afternoon bombardment we had a spotter, a Corsair from Badoeng Strait, and round about 1.30 he told us we had scored two direct hits on the guns of our first target, so we shifted to some field guns. Within a couple of minutes we heard that we had destroyed two of them and holed a tank, which we had not known to be there . . . Less than ten minutes passed before our spotter found some more targets and called for shot on dug-in emplacements and trenches. At this point the left gun of 'A' turret had a flash-back but 'B' opened up and shortly our pilot reported, 'Pretty, *Kenya*, beautiful hit!' Soon after 3 o'clock our ammunition was expended for the day – 321 rounds of 6-inch.

It will be seen from the foregoing that bombardment of shore batteries was not without danger to the bombarding ships, especially with shore gunners as cool under fire and skilful at hitting moving targets as these North Koreans obviously were. Soon after, spotter planes reported troops and vehicles withdrawing from Inchon and the bridgehead area. The troublesome little island of Wolmi-do was captured by a US Marine amphibious force, without casualties. The American admiral expressed his gratitude by signal: 'As Commander of the United Nations Naval Forces under Gen. MacArthur I congratulate and commend British Units under command of Rear Adm. Andrewes for the continued record of sharp shooting at Mokpo and Inchon. Since it is unfortunately necessary to shoot to stay free we are indeed glad to have the sure and fast firing British with us.' Gunnery officers of RN ships were still at this date earning points in the promotion stakes.

As the above account ends:

This was Friday. Less than a week before we had been in Kure with no thought of an invasion, at Inchon or anywhere else. In a few days our whole outlook on the war had changed and *Kenya* had played a major part in what may well be one of the decisive battles of history – the action of the United Nations against an aggressor of the common peace.' (D. Banks, Leading Stoker Mechanic, HMS *Kenya* 1950)

Free-floating mines were a constant danger to Allied ships within a couple of miles of any hostile shore, as the enemy would launch them into fast-flowing rivers to be carried, spinning and bobbing, down to the coast, a trick the communist Chinese learned in the Yangtse against the Nationalist destroyers. They are mentioned frequently in the accounts of sailors who served in Korean waters.

During daylight patrols, the worst hazard was the floating mines which the North Koreans floated down river into the Yellow Sea. Our first encounter with one was in daylight about 3 or 4 miles offshore. Attempts to blow it up giving the pom-poms chance to hone their skills proved abortive, the Oerlikons did not do any better – finally the Gunner, Whale Island stalwart, used the trusty .303 rifle and up she went! Most of the crew who were able to do so, all still wearing life-jackets, watched proceedings with interest and some concern. Shrapnel rained down on the deck needless to say – and, much to others' horror, a signalman dashed out to grab a piece – it was too late to tell him it would be very bloody HOT! It stuck to his hand and I believe he got some punishment to add to his pain.

We did spend some time on the east coast (1951) and operated from Wonsan. We sailed direct from Sasebo in Japan to Wonsan, entering through a swept channel and anchored for the night among ships from several nations and pretty close to the battleship USS *Missouri*. It was sometime during the first or middle watch, I was in my hammock, when the Tannoy burst into life: 'Mine astern, mine astern!' – my first thought was, all watertight doors are closed, if it blows the stern off we forrard have a chance!

The discovery was broadcast to ships in company and the duty watch said that as soon as she received the message, the USS *Missouri* up-anchored and hightailed out to sea at a rate of knots! And who shall blame her?

Her swell created a problem for us, the mine kept bobbing from port to starboard and to have up-anchored and steamed would probably have sucked the mine into our propellers with dire consequences. It was not possible to fend it off with boathooks for fear of striking one of its horns. Finally the leading coxswain I believe, had a brainwave after all kind of ideas were discussed – why not *hose* it away? That is what happened, the searchlights were kept focussed and the fire hoses gradually shifted the mine until it went with the current out to sea.

Years later that incident was highlighted in a *Readers Digest* article as a classic example of lateral thinking!

(C. Harrold, Telegraphist, HMS *Charity* 1951)

After the land war had reached stalemate, truce talks began in July 1951 and dragged on for two years. During this time the naval offensive continued, albeit on a reduced scale, with shore bombardments and stategic air strikes. When the truce was eventually signed the fleet dispersed to its peacetime stations, leaving a lone destroyer or frigate of the Far East fleet anchored off Pyangyong-do on the truce-line, 'swinging round her pick' for two-week spells, on 'Korea patrol'.

After Korea, the next 'big-fleet' action for the Royal Navy took place in 1957 with the inglorious episode of Suez. Many of the same ships were involved, in the same sort of actions of blockade, bombardment, air strikes and amphibious landings. But on this occasion the United States were not leading allies in the enterprise but disapproving senior partners, so that was the end of that. As Britannia's domain continued to shrink, however, there were still plenty of minor incidents to try Jack, in his ageing, increasingly uncomfortable, wartime-utility ships, seemingly never to be refurbished or replaced:

We were sent from the Med to the Persian Gulf to evacuate British nationals from Abadan. We had no air-conditioning and the engine-room mess was unbearably hot. We had to take 16 salt tablets a day being watched by the Leading Stoker. The machinery spaces were almost too hot to enter at 130 degrees plus. Most of my messmates came out in tropical boils; the record was over 100 on one Stoker. I had 4 and had to be very careful sitting down. I still have the scars. We had salt water showers rigged up on the upper deck and then we received complaints from the BP wives about us showering naked. This was ignored as they would have need a telescope to see us. Maybe they had one.

Even the ship's cat had to have shoes made to walk on the deck. What a relief when the *Gambia* came to relieve us.

(B. Whitworth, Stoker Mechanic, HMS *Euryalus* 1951)

Epilogue

Change came, in the end: slowly at first, then with a rapidity that left many long-service men off-balance. It began with the much-vaunted 'New Deal' introduced with the 1956 Naval Estimates and which, apart from an overdue pay rise, promised much and achieved little, aside from bringing in its wake some fairly drastic economies. Over the next two years, much rationalization took place, with wholesale disposal and scrapping of obsolete ships and new or re-built ones emerging from the dockyards. A new generation of ships, together with a new generation of sailors, took the place of those who relate some aspects of their service life in these pages. Theirs is a Navy which has gone; as much a part of history, as the third millenium dawns, as Nelson's. It, and they, should not be forgotten.

When I was joining the ship mentioned earlier, in Devonport dockyard the changes in the 'new post-war Navy' were all about us, some more evident than others. The aircraft-carriers *Albion* and *Bulwark* were undergoing their metamorphosis, as was the cruiser *Cumberland*. The carriers were to become 'assault carriers' and 'commando carriers', mainly for the use of amphibious/helicopter assaults and landings. *Cumberland* lay in a dry-dock hidden from prying (spying?) eyes behind huge screens which completely surrounded the dock and with sentries posted. She was to become Britain's first missile ship. The Seaslug missile first entered service in, I think, 1948 [actually 1956]; was carried thousands of miles across many seas and oceans in RN ships and was only used once, in action and for real, in the Falklands!

Since my time in the Andrew it has changed in so many ways, not all of which I could possibly approve – it's the way of old men! My RN-pensioner uncles used to say they did their stint when 'it was wooden ships and iron men, whereas now . . .' With their 'wooden-wall' training ships, iron discipline and harsh punishments, wickedly bad food and accommodation and three years or longer foreign-service commissions they reckoned, when they were called back for another war after winning the one 'to end all wars' – that things were 'cushy'. It's all relative!

(M. Bree, Leading Writer, HMS *Woolwich* 1954)

Some look back with bitterness . . .

In due course my time came for discharge (1956). As a PO Electrician I had to see some admiral. This enforced interview was unbelievable. Several weeks earlier a 40 per cent pay increase had been announced (to be paid the very day after my final discharge!). Such an increase was seen by some to be a bribe. I saw it as official acknowledgement that the service had been seriously underpaid for some time. Conscription (National Service) was coming to an end and the Services would have to compete for labour like any other employer. There was still little unemployment, which had always been a good recruiting agent! Retaining trained personnel became something of a priority and the Admiral practically begged me to reconsider and stay on. He admitted that lower-deck morale was known to be low and things would rapidly improve. Already CPOs were allowed to wear civilian clothes when going ashore (note, Chiefs – not POs!). Married quarters were going to be provided and the new general service commissions would reduce separation and there would be many other improvements . . . In my particular case (he had been briefed on my service record) there was no doubt I would be a CPO 'practically within days'. I could go to *Collingwood* for the two-year Mechanician course.

Taken together with the 'magnificent' pay rise, service life would become one to be envied! He even asked me what further improvements I would like to see. I did suggest one or two ideas that almost gave him apoplexy – but which, I understand, have since come about. I told him that it all sounded very nice but it was too late to try and convince me.

I have nothing to do with the service these days. I do not belong to the RNA or anything, nor do I want to. I suppose this letter must sound like the ramblings of an embittered old man with a huge chip on his shoulder. Not a bit of it. The Navy did destroy my youth and early manhood – it will not be allowed to spoil my old age as well. I am now utterly indifferent, like the majority of ex-members I meet. I sometimes wonder how they would manage the service now if it was the size it once was. It still cannot attract and retain its manpower – so it is resorting to woman-power!

(J. Crew, Petty Officer Electrician, HMS *Centaur* 1956)

and some with pride . . .

I am what I have always been, a simple man, nothing to speak of or boast about. I was no hero, or man of medals, and did my duty as best I could when I had to. I returned unscathed from my wanderings and was fortunate enough to follow a trade which supported myself, a wife, and three children. I finished up a Leading Stoker, with aspirations of a PO's rate which never occurred. A two-badge Killick. There were worse. I saw some life and yes, death. But in the main, I had a ball. I was never a 'flag-waver', nor even a good Christian, but I was always 'there' when required. Now, I'm long retired, my wife passed-on, my children all married and gone. But I've no regrets. The Navy gave me something invaluable. It taught me the quality of Life and People.

Incidentally, my son is now a serving member and a Chief to boot. I'm proud of him.

(F. Woods, Leading Stoker, HMS *Contest* 1951)

Apart from some modern idiom, that testimonial might have been written by a pre-Dreadnought tar. But not this one:

Well, I was a young ordinary seaman on my first commission. I finished my career as a CPO on *Bulwark*. In my 25 years in the RN there were a lot of changes for the better – maybe. I believe that ships like the *Modeste* made men out of youngsters. I look at the Navy now, I see women prancing in the passageways. Us old 'uns couldn't adapt I suspect. I mean, you couldn't have a dhobey session and come out of the bathroom carrying your dhobey bucket and wearing your flip-flops, towel round your neck and nothing else.

(A. Zammit, St Paul's Bay, Malta GC 1998)

Not without a court-martial, anyway.

Glossary

of lower-deck words and expressions

The RN sailor's everyday speech possessed a rich and inimitable flavour which my correspondents, constrained, perhaps, by the formality of a letter to a stranger, have not always utilized. Or perhaps, like the author, they have simply forgotten . . .

I am grateful to Rick Jolly's excellent *Jackspeak* (Culdrose, 1988) for reminding me of words, phrases and terminology which had for a few years been my own, and I hope the reader will enjoy this brief selection.

All about	astute
All for it	enthusiastic (sometimes used ironically)
Anchor-faced	enthusiastic about the Royal Navy (see *pusser*)
Arse bandit	homosexual
Arseholed	very drunk
Arse over tit	head over heels
At the rush	as fast as possible; faster than 'at the double'
Beer, big eats, bag off and back on board	Jack's ideal run ashore
Bag shanty	a brothel
Baron strangler	a (usually) heterosexual sailor who allowed himself to be entertained ashore by wealthy homosexuals, usually in return for sex
Big eats	pay week meal ashore, invariably steak, egg and chips (see *Blank week*)
Black catter	a messmate who always tops your story; if you have a black cat, his is blacker
Blank week	with sailors paid fortnightly, the week in which pay-day isn't, and Jack is skint
Blow-through	sexual intercourse
Blushing and farting	shy, embarrassed
Bogey Knight	nickname
Boned off	detailed off for an unpopular duty
Brigham Young	nickname
Bubbly	junior ratings' watered rum, or grog

137

Buck Taylor	nickname
Bungy Edwards	nickname
Buzz	messdeck rumour. Common greeting: 'What's the buzz, oppo?'
Cackle the fat	idle chatter
Canteen boat	ship in squadron or flotilla with junior captain; gets all the unpopular jobs
Catch the boat up	contract venereal disease (see *Rose Cottage*)
Chinese wedding cake	rice pudding with currants
Chuffed	very pleased
Clubswinger	Physical Training Instructor (PTI)
Condensing snot	Snoring (engine-room branch)
Crabs	pubic lice, often 'crotch crickets'
Dig in	help yourself – 'fill yer boots'
Dinger Bell	nickname
Dip out	lose out on something
Dip your wick	have sexual intercourse
Dodger Long	nickname
Doggo	ugly, usually ungallantly of a woman
Dolly Gray	nickname
Doofer	half-smoked cigarette ('do fer later')
Drip	moan, complain
Dropped 'is guts (oo's?)	break wind
Duff, up the	pregnant
Dusty Rhodes	nickname
Fanny rat	womanizer
Figgy duff	suet pudding, usually with fruit
Flash as a rat with a gold tooth	very flash
Flog yer log	masturbate
Friday while	long weekend leave (Friday while Monday)
Gannet	a greedy, left-over-eating rating
Gash	surplus to requirements, messdeck waste
Gens (submarines)	General Service, i.e. surface Navy
Go round the buoy	repeat, take a second helping
Gobbler's gulch	area between stocking tops and suspender belt
Goffer	big breaking wave, fruit-flavoured soft drink
Green rub	unjust treatment, detailing, draft etc.
Half a dogwatch	short time, usually derogatory of a rating's comparative lack of service
Hang out of	cohabit with a woman
Hard shit!	bad luck

Head down	sleep: 'Get your head down'
Herrings in	herrings in tomato sauce (HITS)
Hoggin	the sea
Homeward bounders	large, untidy, hurried stitches
Honk (your ring up)	be violently sick
Hooky	a leading hand, from his anchor rank badge
Jack Dusty	a supply rating
Jack Strop	a bellicose rating
Jacksie	anus
Jan/Janner	a West Country rating
Jaunty	the Master-at-Arms
Jig-a-jig	brothel visit
Jimmy/Jimmy the One	First Lieutenant
Jockanese	English spoken with impenetrable Glasgow accent, frequently by bosun's mates
Jumper Cross	nickname
Killick	another word for leading hand (see *Hooky*)
Kitty Wells	nickname
'kin 'ell!	abbreviated expostulation
Knacker crackers	beefy female thighs
Knocker White	nickname
Knuckle bosun	bellicose rating given to fisticuffs
Kye	cocoa made from grated block of dark, unsweetened chocolate. Favoured nightwatch drink
Lash-up	generous hospitality, also makeshift (and unsatisfactory) arrangement.
Laughing gear	mouth
Lazy lob	partial erection
Lead on MacDick	undiscriminating fornicator (see *Fanny rat*)
Like a one-armed paperhanger with crabs	frantic and ill-coordinated activity
Lob on	an erection
Mankey	filthy
Messdeck dodger	messdeck sweeper or cleaner
Mick	hammock ('sling me mick')
Muff diver	rating given to oral intercourse
Muscle bosun	PTI, or body-builder rating
Musical fruit	baked beans or pusser's peas
Nap hand	unlucky contracting of both gonorrhoea and syphilis from same source, sometimes accompanied by pubic lice ('crutch

	crickets') for good measure (see *Rose Cottage*)
Navy cake	homosexual sailor
Neaters	unwatered rum, issued to chief and petty officers
North-easter	rating having no money due to him at pay-muster has a north-easter (NE: Not Entitled)
Nutty	any chocolate or sweets, whether or not containing nuts
Oggie	Cornish pastie, or native of Cornwall
Old ships	old shipmate, someone previously served with
Oppo	close chum. From 'opposite number', rating with the same job as oneself in another watch
Out of watch	'getting a bit' with a lady not one's wife
'Out pipes!'	pipe made at end of stand-easy, order to resume work
Over the wall	spell in detention quarters
Party	sailor's steady girl-friend
Pea-do	naval long service and good conduct medal awarded after 15 years (origin obscure)
Phoo-phoo	talcum powder
Pi-r-squared rating	one who can do sums, studious (derogatory)
Pierhead jump	draft at very short notice
Pissed off	fed-up
Piss flap	buttoned flap in lieu of flies on sailors' trousers
Plushers/plussers	rum remaining in tub after issue made
Porridge guns	bagpipes
Potmess	makeshift messdeck stew. Also anything muddled or messed-up
Pox doctor's clerk (the luck of a)	very lucky – the pox-doctor's clerk having access to the files and knowing which ladies were infected
Pusher	another term for girl-friend (see *Party*)
Pusser	ship's Supply Officer (Purser), also anyone or anything formal, correct and navy-style
Quack	medical officer
Quick burn	rapidly and slyly smoked cigarette
Quiet number	cushy job
Rattle, in the	up on a disciplinary charge

Red lead	tinned tomato
Ring piece	anus
Ring stinger	hot curry
Roof rats	flight-deck gang
Rose Cottage	venereal disease ward or clinic
Royal	sailor's name for Royal Marine, but more often 'bootneck'
Rug rat	small child
Rum bosun	rating who draws the rum ration for his mess and serves it out
Rum rat	rating with an excessive craving for rum
Scran	food
Scran-bag	personal kit found 'sculling about' on the messdeck was put in the scran-bag, to be redeemed on payment of an inch of pusser's hard soap
Soapy Watson	nickname
Spasm chasm	vagina
Spithead pheasant	kipper
Split-arse mechanic	female
Square rig	junior ratings' uniform
Squeeze up	experience gonorrhoea symptoms
Stamps	of no importance or status
Stonker	erection
Straight rush	roast meat and vegetables
Stroll on!	expression of incredulity
Sweating neaters	very anxious state ('neaters': neat rum)
Swain	Coxswain (senior rate of a small warship)
Tailor-made	manufactured cigarette, as opposed to hand-rolled
Thickers	condensed milk
Tickler	Navy-issue cigarette tobacco
Tiddley	smart, as in 'tiddley suit', No. 1 uniform
Tiffy	Artificer
Timber Woods	nickname
Toggle and two	male genitalia
Torpoint chicken	'built like a Torpoint chicken – all prick and toenails'
Townie	shipmate with the same home town
Tram smash	bacon and tinned tomato
Tug Wilson	nickname
Twelve	continuous service engagement of 12 years.

	'Roll on my f***ing twelve!' heard everywhere, at any time, on the lower deck
Ullage	residue in a barrel, also a worthless individual or group
Up homers	family hospitality extended to Jack in foreign ports
Up the line	usually, home – 'going up the line': proceeding on leave
Upside-down head	a bald sailor with a beard
Wanchai burberry	a cheap oiled-paper and bamboo umbrella on sale everywhere in Hong Kong; also known as a 'dollar brolly'
Warming the bell	returning aboard only just in time; risking being 'adrift'
Watch on stop on	continuous duty without relief
Weed, weejie	to have a weed or a weejie on is to be angry
Wet as a scrubber	description of useless individual
Wiggy Bennet	nickname
Wind yer neck in!	shut up!
Winger	another word for 'oppo'
Wood butcher	Carpenter or 'Chippie'
Wrap up	give up doing or saying something
Yaffle	eat greedily
Yodel in a bucket	be seasick
You-can't bend-it	vague reference, 'thingummy', how's-your-father

Notes

INTRODUCTION

1. Adm. Sir Frank Twiss KCB, KCVO, DSC.
2. AF Sir Peter Hill-Norton GCB.
3. In a Parliamentary reply (*Hansard*, June 1953) it was revealed that in some branches, re-engagement rates prior to the Retention Order keeping on time-expired ratings for a further 18 months, ran at 4 per cent. Following the Order, when ratings affected would have had only the balance of eight and a half years to serve for pension, the re-engagement rate rose to a mere 7 per cent. It was noted with some bitterness that time-expired men in the Army were compulsorily retained for six months and those in the Royal Air Force for three months during the same emergency, and the lower deck believed, rightly or wrongly, that this was another Admiralty 'dirty trick' aimed at covering a shortage of senior rates.
4. Adm. Sir Frank Twiss.

CHAPTER ONE

1. A very grown-up version of the child's game of Ludo.

2. A 'three-badge' AB, Stoker etc. was one who had served long enough in a career of undetected crime to have accrued the maximum number of long service and good conduct chevrons (while avoiding promotion) awarded after four, eight and twelve years' service, and was more usually known as 'Stripey'. This appellation was not accorded to leading hands and petty officers who had rank badges to go with the stripes.
3. On the lower deck, commonly-used nickname for the Royal Navy, said to be after one Lt. Andrew Miller, a very successful eighteenth-century press-gang officer.
4. Circular armoured shield below an upper deck gun-turret protecting the ammunition hoist. 'A' is the foremost turret in a 4-turret ship, the others being, from forward, 'B', 'X' and 'Y'.
5. Perhaps because of those restrictions, *Arethusa* was actually classed as a light cruiser.
6. An unofficial laundry service for large, bulky items of kit such as hammocks and blankets, provided, for a consideration and in their off-duty time, by a pair of entrepreneurs who were often engine-room ratings with access to

the drying facilities of boiler-rooms.

7. Traditional, and horribly inconvenient, dress of the common sailor, in which everything went over the head but the trousers. Worn by leading hands and below of the seaman, communications and stoker branches. Compare with the 'fore and aft' rig of peaked cap, conventional buttoned jacket and collar and tie worn by chief and petty officers and, at this date, 'miscellaneous' ratings such as cooks, officers' stewards, writers etc.

CHAPTER TWO

1. *The Royal Navy since 1945* A. Cecil Hampshire, London, William Kimber, 1975.
2. Capt. John Wells, CBE, DSC, RN.
3. *Nelson's Blood* Capt. James Pack OBE, RN, Stroud, Sutton Publishing Ltd, 1995.
4. This was one of those 'well-known facts' beloved of the lower deck. In reality the Admiralty purchased its rum supplies like everybody else.
5. The author begs to be excused supplying the missing word. Suffice to say that this was a truly revolting breakfast dish of a plate of minced beef with a fried egg eyeing one liquidly from its centre.

CHAPTER THREE

1. Which is not to say that the old skills were no longer needed. The author, when second coxswain ('scratcher') of a submarine remote from a dockyard, was ordered to replace a worn periscope wire. This hot and filthy task was accomplished after some ten hours' labour, much of it bent double in the bilges with an oily cat's-cradle of wire and pulleys and much blood-stained splicing of steel rope. It earned on completion the triple tot of whisky from the wardroom wine-locker traditional for a wire-change.
2. Adm. Sir Frank Twiss.
3. On watch one day in the operations room when an aircraft ploughed into the crash barrier on the flight-deck below, the author narrowly escaped decapitation from a large, jagged shard of broken propeller which hurtled through a carelessly-open scuttle and crashed into the opposite bulkhead – escaped providentially by leaning across the plotting table to update a plot at the precise moment.
4. Capt. Wells's *The Royal Navy* contains the following account by one AS Minchin concerning Winston Churchill as First Lord. The latter frequently visited ships in harbour without prior notice, a practice which made him unpopular with senior officers. He appeared aboard *Invincible* one Sunday afternoon to find ratings rigging stages preparatory to painting ship. According to Minchin: 'the gunnery officer met him at the gangway and Winston

wanted to know why the men were working on a Sunday. He was told: "On orders from the Commander."

"Where is the Commander?" demanded Winston.

"Ashore, sir."

"Where is the Captain?"

"Ashore, sir."

Anyway they brought us in out of it and the Skipper had to go to the Admiral's quarters the following day and he made a report.'

The sailors, at least, adored Winston.

CHAPTER FOUR

1. Henry Capper, quoted by Baynham in *Men from the Dreadnoughts*, London, Hutchinson, 1976.

2. The 'overnight' aspect is illustrated by an instance known to the author when an extension of the scheme further promoted the warrant officers (now known as 'Branch List' officers) according to their length of service in warrant rank. An elderly commissioned boatswain 'did rounds' of the messdecks one evening as Officer of the Day, and appeared at 'Both Watches of the Hands' the next morning, looking slightly self-conscious as well he might, as a full-blown lieutenant commander, his single gold-lace ring increased to two-and-a-half.

3. Lower deck candidates for commission were so called from the wooden-wall era, with the smartest

seamen manning the upper yards when working sail. Officially, a CW candidate became an upper-yardman only when, and if, he got as far as training at HMS *Hawke*.

4. AF Sir Edward Ashmore in *The Battle and the Breeze*, Stroud, Sutton, 1997.

5. Named after the Asian fig tree. An impromptu 'run ashore' in a ship's boat, usually at a remote tropical beach, for bathing and picnicking. A generous stock of beer was a prerequisite.

6. *Dry Ginger*, the biography of AF Sir Michael Le Fanu GCB, DSC, by Richard Baker, London, W.H. Allen, 1977.

CHAPTER FIVE

1. Dame Agnes Weston (1840–1911). Spinster daughter of a successful barrister and a fervent temperance crusader, devoted her life to those she called 'my bluejackets'. Established the famous Sailors Rest hostels at Portsmouth, Devonport and Keyham, Plymouth where Jack could get a cheap, clean bed even, or especially, when too drunk to return on board. The Rests were always known as 'Aggie's'.

2. In a destroyer cruising the West Indies a certain Scots AB, trading on this handicrafts tradition, spent all his dogwatches pegging a rug of coloured wool from one of those 'Jester' kits popular at the time, forswearing all runs ashore. Before the ship returned to

Devonport the rug was completed, all but the hessian backing. 'Jock' then went round the messdecks buying up tins of duty-free ration tobacco from those with no use for it, accumulating some four pounds weight. This he stuffed between rug and backing, smoothed all flat, rolled it up and wrapped it in brown paper and string. He smuggled it successfully past the policeman on the dockyard gate, who contented himself by thrusting a hand down the middle of the roll.

3. Originally a holiday from working ship to allow men to make and mend their clothing. Later the name given to an afternoon off.

CHAPTER SIX

1. See *Invergordon Scapegoat*, Alan Coles, Stroud, Sutton, 1993.
2. See the author's *Smuggling*, David & Charles, Newton Abbot 1973.

CHAPTER SEVEN

1. An example being the famous Field Gun competition at the annual Royal Tournament, fought out between the three port divisions plus the Fleet Air Arm.
2. Ship's police, i.e. leading patrolman, regulating petty officer, master-at-arms, marine corporal of the gangway. The name 'Crusher' is thought to derive from the crushing under the boot-soles of cockroaches

making free of the sleeping messdeck when calling the hands.

3. A Russian football team who toured western Europe in the late 1940s, winning most of their matches and scoring, as well as goals, propaganda points for the Soviet regime.
4. The Royal Naval Hospitals at Haslar, Gosport and Stonehouse, Plymouth.
5. Leading hand, so called from the killick or small admiralty-pattern anchor worn as a rank badge on the left sleeve.
6. Capt. Frank Shaw, *The Navy of Tomorrow*, London, Werner Laurie, 1950.
7. Royal yacht crew uniform was the same as general service except that badges were white instead of red; a flash was worn at the shoulder reading 'Royal Yacht' with a crown; bell-bottom trousers of junior rates had a black silk bow at the waist behind, visible because the yachtie sailor's jumper was tucked into his trousers after the fashion of a Victorian bluejacket and, of course, his hat sported a cap-tally emblazoned 'HMRY BRITANNIA' with the royal crown in gold wire.

CHAPTER EIGHT

1. An exception to this rule were the two boys' training establishments of HMS *Ganges* at Shotley and *St Vincent* at Gosport, where Boy Seamen and Boy Signalmen/ Telegraphists were trained

together but followed separate syllabuses.

2. Quoted in Wells, *The Royal Navy*.
3. Ibid. page 223.
4. Commissioned or warrant gunners who had passed the Long Course, and whose entry in the Navy List was distinguished by a small dagger-like symbol.

CHAPTER NINE

1. Hampshire, *The Royal Navy since 1945*.
2. Quoted in *The Navy, 1939 to the Present Day*, Max Arthur, Hodder & Stoughton, 1997.
3. The author, in a conversation many years later with one of these 'volunteers', an ordnance artificer, was told of a suggestion by a senior officer (unnamed) at Shanghai that the aircraft should make a low-level pass alongside the frigate to allow the men to jump out into the river. He was taken aside by a white-faced medical officer to have explained to him in graphic detail what happens to a human body striking water at 60 miles per hour, and the suggestion was withdrawn.
4. To Max Arthur, recorded in his *The Navy, 1939 to the Present Day*, Hodder & Stoughton, 1997.
5. After salvage, an enquiry established that her loss was the direct result of a trifling, but in the event deadly, piece of slapdashery on the part of dockyard painters who had clogged with paint a vital 'tell-tale' cock designed to reveal the presence of seawater in the forward torpedo tubes. When during the trials the cock was opened and emitted no water, it was wrongly assumed that the bow-cap of the tube was shut and the tube dry. The inner door was opened and the sea rushed in.

After the event, all tube doors were fitted with an extra clip which had to be partially unscrewed before removal; this allowed an inboard door to open a fraction while still restrained, when a flooded tube would become obvious to a torpedoman as his boots filled with water. This simple device was known as the 'Thetis clip'.

6. From the *Japan News* dated 29 September 1950: 'The Communist China news agency reported yesterday that an American warship shelled a Chinese merchant vessel in the Yellow Sea off Shantung Peninsular on 21 September . . . The report said the American warship forced the merchant vessel to stop, drew alongside and questioned the crew and passengers including 4 women and 2 children.'

A starshell is, of course, a pyrotechnic used to illuminate a target and is not a missile.

A common error in those early days of radar plotting was to take the range and bearing of a target too frequently, when the inbuilt inaccuracies of the radar would tend to give false readings of the speed of a slow-moving target such as a motorised junk.

Bibliography

In addition to the many primary sources in the form of letters, audio-tapes and telephone conversations which make up the bulk of this book, I have drawn to a greater or lesser degree upon the following published works:

Arthur, Max, *The Navy, 1939 to the Present Day*, London, Hodder & Stoughton, 1997.

Ashmore, Sir Edward, Adm. of the Fleet, *The Battle and the Breeze*, Stroud, Sutton Publishing Ltd, 1997.

Baker, Richard, *Dry Ginger* (Biography of Adm. of the Fleet Sir Michael le Fanu), London, W.H. Allen, 1977.

Baynham, Henry, *Men from the Dreadnoughts*, London, Hutchinson, 1976.

Divine, David, *Mutiny at Invergordon*, London, MacDonald, 1970.

Glenton, Robert, *The Royal Oak Affair*, London, Lee Cooper, 1991.

Gray, Edwyn, *Few Survived*, London, Lee Cooper, 1986.

Hampshire, A. Cecil, *The Royal Navy since 1945*, London, William Kimber, 1975.

Jolly, Rick, *Jackspeak, a Guide to Royal Navy Slanguage*, Culdrose, 1988.

Pack, Capt. James, RN, *Nelson's Blood, The Story of Naval Rum*, Emsworth, 1982.

Shaw, Capt. Frank, *The Navy of Tomorrow*, London, Werner Laurie, 1950.

'Tackline', *Holiday Sailor*, London, Hollis & Carter, 1945 ('Tackline' = pseudonym).

Twiss, Adm. Sir Frank, *Social Change in the Royal Navy 1924–70*, Stroud, Sutton Publishing Ltd, 1996.

Wells, Capt. John, RN, *The Royal Navy 1870 to 1982*, Stroud, Sutton Publishing Ltd, 1994.

Wigby, Frederick, *Stoker – Royal Navy*, Edinburgh, Blackwood, 1967.

Index

Plate numbers and illustration page numbers are in italics